To:

....

From:

....

Consider the
LILIES

Published by iDisciple Publishing, 2555 Northwinds Parkway, Alpharetta, GA 30009
In association with WTA Media, Franklin, TN

ISBN: 978-0-578-85578-3

Written by Shari Rigby

Content Development/Editing by Robert Noland.

Cover and Layout design by Annabelle Grobler.

Consider the LILIES

40-DAY DEVOTIONAL

*Find purpose in an
ever-changing culture.*

SHARI RIGBY

Contents

Contents

Consider the lilies,
how they grow:
they neither toil nor spin;
and yet I say to you,
even Solomon in all his glory
was not arrayed like one of these.

~LUKE 12:27 NKJV~

From Shari

Hello sister! I'm so thrilled that you have decided to join me in spending time with the Lord for the next forty days by digging deep into His Word and reflecting on how you were created to grow, just like the lilies of the valley.

When I launched into writing, I was immediately thrust into a new season of life, moving across the country from California to Georgia, caretaking my elderly parents, and then dealing with the loss of my mother, all before the holidays in the tumultuous year of 2020. Yet, honestly, every day was truly a labor of love between me and Jesus, our Kinsman Redeemer. On a typical morning, I would rise early, grab my coffee, sit on the sofa, and cry out to the Lord to fill me with His message. Often with tears streaming down my face, arms in the air, hands lifted high, I would express my need for the Holy Spirit's power.

From that experience, He gave me these love letters—daily devotions to His daughters to inspire, encourage, and empower us so we can grow roots as we experience a deeper relationship with Jesus. The Father showed up over and over again, offering me His mercy and grace, providing me with a message that I pray you will consume and incorporate into your daily routine. Please know that I love you and believe that you are one of the Women in my World, part of the colony of God's beautiful lilies rising up and using our voices to glorify His kingdom.

As you work through the next 40 days, I pray the words from Numbers 6:24-26 over you, *"The Lord bless you and keep you; The Lord make His face shine upon you, And be gracious to you; The Lord lift up His countenance upon you, And give you peace"* (NKJV).

Dig in, Sisters!

Day 1

TOILING AND SPINNING

The book of Ecclesiastes begins with the subtitle "The Futility of all Endeavor," penned by the great King Solomon. Chosen over his brothers by God and his father King David, he was given power, wisdom, fame, fortune, and wealth. He was highly favored, giving him the utmost respect of the people; and God gave him the honor and authority to build the Temple. Yet the man who had it all wrote about the human experience of toiling and spinning for everything under the sun only to watch everything pass away.

I turned my head and saw yet another wisp of smoke on its way to nothingness: a solitary person, completely alone—no children, no family, no friends—yet working obsessively late into the night, compulsively greedy for more and more, never bothering to ask, "Why am I working like a dog, never having any fun? And who cares?" More smoke. A bad business. (Ecclesiastes 4:7-8 MSG)

Solomon took the throne during a time of abundance, and as women today, we too have come into a time of affluence and prosperity. It is certainly a great time in history to be a woman. Female politicians now lead nations. Women teach the Bible and lead ministries, sharing the Gospel globally. In entertainment, women are creating incredible multi-million-dollar productions that employ thousands of people. The top three youngest billionaires are now all females. Women seem to be taking over the world!

However, while women continue to make strides like never before, we still struggle to find our way. There is a deep discontentment in our collective spirit. So many are profoundly dissatisfied with life just like Solomon wrote in today's passage. Suicide and depression are at all-time highs and climbing. Anxiety and fear are leading to dramatic increases in substance addiction. We are constantly comparing ourselves to others, obsessing over social media, causing us to toil and spin out of control, desperately trying to find identity and purpose.

So what is the cause of all this discontent amongst advancement? How can we find peace in prosperity? We must stop looking to the right and the left and instead keep our eyes, our focus, on the One who created us, going from confusion to clarity knowing we are enough in our relationship with the Creator of the universe. We must identify with Him first, not the ever-changing world. Stop seeking people's approval and walk in the favor according to God's plan set before us.

And let us run with endurance the race God has set before us. We do this by keeping our eyes on Jesus, the champion who initiates and perfects our faith.

Hebrews 12:1-2 NLT

Roots

In the struggles we discussed today, which ones are specifically affecting you in your personal strength and growth?

_____

_____

_____

_____

_____

_____

Blooms

In the circumstances you're walking through right now, where do you need to change course, take your eyes off others, and look to Christ alone?

_____

_____

_____

_____

_____

_____

Prayer

"Heavenly Father, help me to constantly surrender my toiling and spinning to You. When I begin to strive and struggle, give me the strength to lift my head and place my eyes only on You. In Jesus' name, amen."

Today offers
the greatest opportunity
in history
to be a woman!

GROWN IN GLORY

Growing up, I dreamt I could be anything I set my mind and heart to be, from a superhero to a model, a rock star to a cowgirl, a police officer to a princess, an actress to a wife and mom. In a moment, I could go from flying solo high in the sky to walking down the aisle toward my Prince Charming. Imagining fame and glory in the whos and whats of this world, I always believed my possibilities were endless.

But growing up, those dreams turned to a mirage, as I got lost in a dry, empty, lonely world as vast as the Sahara Desert. As far as I could see there were only rolling hills of sunbaked sand where nothing survived. Lost and tossed from one place to the next, I was still seeking those childhood fantasies but in all the wrong places. I longed to grow in glory the way I had pretended as a young girl. I found myself withering away in the midst of thorns, trapped and bruised by the brambles all around me.

> *"Look at the birds of the sky, that they do not sow, nor reap, nor gather crops into barns, and yet your heavenly Father feeds them. Are you not much more important than they? And which of you by worrying can add a single day to his life's span? And why are you worried about clothing?*

Notice how the lilies of the field grow; they do not labor nor do they spin thread for cloth, yet I say to you that not even Solomon in all his glory clothed himself like one of these."

Jesus in Matthew 6:26-29

After many years of "toil and spin," unable to grow on my own in elusive glory, I met the Creator of the lily, the One who clothes the eye-catching, breathtaking, hearty flowers that flourish in the fields. But first, I had to know Him personally as the Master Gardener. I had to give my life fully to Christ. I had to dig deep in His Word, digesting the stories about ordinary people enabled to do extraordinary things to bring *Him* glory. I soon discovered the only way to *grow in glory* is to *grow in Christ,* not in the things of this world.

Like the gardener, God looks for the best environment in rich soil with a balance of nutrients and proper water flow; digging deep, offering ample space for the bulb to grow and thrive, blooming season after season over its lifetime. Like the lily, we must take root where we are planted so we can flourish. Whether we become a model, rock star, cowgirl, police officer, princess, actress, wife and mom, or whatever life passion we choose wherever He plants us, to truly follow Christ is to grow in His glory.

Roots

When you first came to Christ, what and/or whom did God most use to help you get properly planted?

_____

_____

_____

_____

_____

Blooms

When you first came to Christ, what was the single biggest change you faced to begin your growth?

_____

_____

_____

_____

_____

Prayer

"Master Gardener, thank You for the careful manner in which You planted me to grow in Your glory. Thank You for the countless ways You have taken care of me. Help me to keep growing in You for Your glory. In Jesus' name, amen."

The only way to grow
in glory is to grow
in Christ, not in the
things of the world.

Day 3

DIVINE DESIGN

One of the two main types of lilies from the genus *Lilium* is known as "true lilies," representing at least one hundred species. The many hybrids make for countless varieties of the garden lily. These delicate yet hearty flowers offer an amazing bouquet of visual beauty to any garden or field. The lily is the perfect flower to plant for optimal artistry because they are able to offer their splendor from early spring to first frost.

Planting any type of lily is like creating a canvas of color. Their pallet ranges from bold colors to a white as pure as fresh fallen snow. Lilies can have an intoxicating fragrance or very little aroma. With so many unique shapes and sizes, no wonder the lily is one of the most noted flowers in the Bible with fifteen distinct references. Their visual beauty and strong fortitude are a powerful metaphor for how we as women are also designed by the ultimate Botanist.

Like lilies, God's daughters are captivating, aromatic, diverse, and vibrant. Therefore, we must celebrate one another's unique qualities, uniting together to further His kingdom. We also must embrace how we have been divinely designed. The closer we grow in our

relationship with Christ, the better we understand ourselves as well as the other women with whom He has planted us to grow. Our heavenly Father wants us to *celebrate* our individualism while encouraging one another to *cultivate* who He has made us to be.

As I have grown in my relationship with the Lord, I have come to understand how much He loves *all of me*. As the Artist, He penciled in every hair on my head, shadowed the line of my oval face, calculated my height, and mixed the greens and yellows of my eyes. He chose the inner ingredients of my soul that make me who I am and how I love others. As the King of the world, He crafted me as His daughter, so I must seek to use *all of me* to glorify Him and His kingdom.

Take some time to study your divine design, your unique qualities as a woman, and how He handcrafted you to fit into creation. God wants to use all of you, but first you must come to view yourself through the eyes of Christ. As His cherished and treasured daughter, He looks upon you as beautiful, powerful, and created for a purpose. He fashioned you in His image, so how could you be anything less?

Instead of looking at the fashions, walk out into the fields and look at the wildflowers. They never primp or shop, but have you ever seen color and design quite like it? The ten best-dressed women in the country look shabby alongside them.

Matthew 6:28-29 MSG (adapted)

Roots

What internal strengths and qualities has God placed inside you that uniquely form who you are?

_____

_____

_____

_____

Blooms

What is your one most striking external quality God has given you that people tend to compliment or comment on?

_____

_____

_____

_____

Prayer

"Divine Designer, thank You for the metaphor of the lily as an example of how You see me. Thank You for the unique and personal way You fashioned me inside and out. Please help me to see all of me as You do so I may use all of me for You. In Jesus' name, amen."

My Creator has divinely

designed me

to offer all I am

to show the beauty

of all He is!

COMMUNITY IN COLONIES

The Wolf Creek Trout Lily Preserve can be found along the East Coast from Maryland to Florida and inland west as far as Kentucky, Tennessee, and Alabama. Botanists report this particular lily species could have been growing in this expansive region for thousands of years. This flower has survived the encroachment of humans since America began its colonization. Some of these colonies cover up to ten acres with one hundred plants per square foot. Because of their strength and unity in growing together, these lilies have not only survived the centuries but have thrived.

No coincidence that populations of these flowering plants are known by the same word as people groups. One of Merriam Webster's definitions for *colony* is: "a group of individuals with common characteristics or interests situated in close association." As women who follow Christ, He is our "common characteristic and interest that situates us in close association." This is exactly why when Christian women meet for the first time, we can have an immediate common foundation and heart connection. We are indeed a flowering colony in Christ!

Over the years I have come to understand that the Lord is a God of relationships. So many times I have seen how He has grafted me into His own colonies. When He connects any of us in this way, these become the people that "we do life with" to navigate callings, family, friends, careers, and all our circles of influence.

The Women in Our World are the other lilies in the field growing near us, around us, and connected to us. The God of the lily in its beautiful, breathtaking extensive colonies is our God, too.

Always be humble and gentle. Be patient with each other, making allowance for each other's faults because of your love. Make every effort to keep yourselves united in the Spirit, binding yourselves together with peace. For there is one body and one Spirit, just as you have been called to one glorious hope for the future.

Ephesians 4:2-4 NLT

The Message Bible offers verses 4 and 6 of Ephesians 4 as: *You were all called to travel on the same road and in the same direction, so stay together, both outwardly and inwardly. . . . Everything you are and think and do is permeated with Oneness.*

With the women in your own circles, you walk together through the good and the bad because you *know* you are traveling on the same road in the same direction. You stay together by praying for one another, serving, and supporting each other. With the women in your colony, you can sense you are "permeated with Oneness" in Christ.

Roots

When you first began to follow Christ, who were the women God placed in your life to help you find your place in His colony?

_____

_____

_____

_____

Blooms

Today, who are the women that God has given you to help find their place in His colony?

_____

_____

_____

_____

Today, who are the women that God has placed around you to keep you strong in His colony?

_____

_____

_____

_____

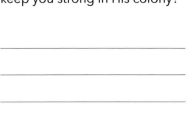

Prayer

"Heavenly Father, thank You for the beautiful, amazing colony You have placed me inside to grow and bloom, to support and strengthen my sisters. Guide me in my ministry among the women in my world to show and share You with those who desperately need Your life in theirs. In Jesus' name, amen."

I am in
Christ's colony
permeated with
Oneness!

CLOTHED IN COLOR

In Luke 12:27, Jesus offered the great King Solomon as the closest comparison to the lily in being clothed in all his glory. Regarded as one of the greatest kings of all time, he had it all—God's blessing, wisdom, extraordinary wealth, vast amounts of land, a huge family, and anything he desired.

King Solomon's palace was another expression of his great wealth. 1 Kings 7 describes that every wall and ceiling were made of wood from the Cedar of Lebanon tree, decorated with precious metals, brilliant stones, and rich woods offering visual splendor. Tables, chairs, utensils, and the like were made of pure gold. The large bronze pillars were fashioned with capitals. Chain work that sat on their tops was adorned with pomegranate design finished off with impressions of the lily.

Just imagine the magnificent artwork that gave life to his palace. I envision murals telling the remarkable stories of God, King David, the Mighty Men, and the beauty of the Holy Land. Colorful fabrics must have bordered the windows, covered the beds, and accessorized the living quarters, breathtaking and bold in appearance.

With such lavish living quarters for him and his family, then just as Jesus said, Solomon must have been adorned in such riches, clothed in eye-catching and audacious colors. Ushered into the throne room and into the presence of the king, everyone could see Solomon's garments told of his wealth and stature.

Rich colors, fine fabrics, pure fragrances, lustrous metals, and brilliant stones identified the prestigious then, and to this day, the wealthy still set themselves apart by incorporating these items of luxury into their lives as well. And what woman doesn't love beautiful clothing, striking and stunning, setting us apart from others as we walk into a room? But as the Creator, God knew humans would be intoxicated with the visual aspect of life. And why not? After all, God created beauty, and we are drawn to His creation.

> *Charm is deceitful and beauty is vain, But a*
> *woman who fears the Lord, she shall be praised.*
>
> Proverbs 31:30

We know from experience that this verse is true, so how do we continue to shine like the lily, bold and radiant in all its color through *every* season of our lives?

We must take heart in the preparation season. Like the grand Gardener He is, God provides us with rich food to feast on in His Word, along with the perfect amount of light and warmth to sit in His presence. So when He whispers, "It's time," we can explode through the soil, bloom in the diverse, striking colors He crafted each one of us to have. Not because of the showy fabric with which we clothe our bodies, but because our hearts and spirits are strong, full of wisdom and power to shine brightly for the world to see.

Sisters, the lily rests in the truth that to be bold, brilliant, and breath-taking, it must be fed from the inside out. **Together,** let's discover how God wants to clothe us in color, by His hand, in His ways.

Roots

What character qualities do you most want God to develop and grow in your heart and spirit?

_____

_____

_____

_____

Blooms

What internal attributes have people affirmed that they see in you?

_____

_____

_____

_____

Prayer

"Glorious One, thank You for the gift of beauty in the world You created. But thank You that as human beauty fades, You allow us to become even more beautiful in our hearts and spirits by displaying Your love and grace in our lives. In Jesus' name, amen."

Be certain
your heart is ready
when God whispers,
"It's time."

BORN TO BLOOM

*I will be like the dew to Israel; He will blossom like the lily,
And he will take root like the cedars of Lebanon.*

Hosea 14:5

God, the most artistic, visual Storyteller of all, the Master Planner of the universe, created you for Himself, for a purpose. That is the very reason the Bible begins with the creation of the world, of everything He called into existence, including the lilies. He gave life, planting these amazing flowers in all the countless places where they were born to bloom, to dig deep and blossom in beauty.

The lily is found throughout the Bible as a flower as well as a metaphor. As we talked about yesterday, the lily was incorporated into the design of the bronze pillars of King Solomon's palace. The lily was also part of the portrait created to represent Israel and the promise of restoration. The bold rich colors, elaborate shapes, spectacular height, and powerful fragrance symbolized what Israel would look like to the world. Make no mistake that God is the Artist who knows how to captivate the eye by the exterior attributes of His creation.

Incredible how, like the lily, we too have been created with splendor in the image of the Creator. Of course, the exterior becomes even more

dazzling as the interior pours forth the alluring fragrance within us to represent Christ. He plants us in places that He knows will provide the richest soil in which we can bloom. But first, we must go through the process of taking root.

Gardeners and botanists offer their advice on the importance of planting lily bulbs for optimal growth to ensure blooms that will return year after year. Taking in their well-laid instructions for planting, I have seen the many similarities between our lives and the lily.

The lily must be planted in the:

1. Right place
   - For deep rich soil.
   - For proper hydration and water flow.
   - With lots of sun.
   - To offer long life.

2. Right space
   - With room for the roots to spread out.
   - Offering stability to stand tall and strong.
   - For depth to keep the bulb cool when faced with hot temperatures.
   - Before the first freeze of winter to establish roots and produce spring blooms.

You were created and born to stand tall, to show off with your brilliant showy colors, and be fruitful in your life. You were born to bloom!

Roots

Comparing your current spiritual environment to the analogy of the lily's "right space" and "right place," is there anything in your life that may be hurting or stunting your maturity and stability?

_____

_____

_____

_____

_____

Blooms

Comparing your current spiritual environment to the analogy of the lily's "right space" and "right place," what factors in your life are encouraging and nurturing you to grow and bloom?

_____

_____

_____

_____

_____

Prayer

"Heavenly Father, show me the changes I need to make to strengthen my roots to grow in You. Help me to stay in the right space and the right place to bloom in all the ways You designed me when You shaped and formed me. In Jesus' name, amen."

Your season

to bloom

has arrived!

Day 7

Digging Deeper - ONE

In His World

Let all creation sing! Yesterday, we discovered the beauty of being *born to bloom* and the similarities of our lives and the lily. Today, take your devotional time outside. Look around and soak in the beauty surrounding you. Wouldn't it be inspiring to take on a project to plant your own lilies as a part of going through this devotional?

First, find the perfect spot that offers the right place and the right space to plant your own lilies. When you locate where you would like your flowers to grow, sit next to the area you have chosen and go through the next two sections of today's devotional.

Allow this project to be a spiritual marker in your own walk with Christ as you take part in His creation and inspire your own growth to bloom in new ways. Imagine the many years you can come back to this spot again and again to remember what the Lord spoke to you in this season and throughout your many seasons of blooming for His glory. Just like your lilies.

In His Worship

As you sit in the midst of God's creation at the site of your lily-planting project, praise Him for His creation. Worship Him for the blessing of life, beauty, and strength. Thank Him for His gift of allowing you to bloom where you've been planted.

Pray and talk with the Lord about the connection between your life and the lilies you are about to plant. Ask Him to reveal truths to you as you watch your lilies go through the rooting season, forming colonies below to prepare for the spring bloom. Is there a certain lily that you relate to? One that is bold in color and intoxicating in fragrance or a classic white with the alluring smells of spring? Choose one that visually represents you. As you finish praying, read the passage provided below.

In His Word

The desert and dry land will become happy; the desert will be glad and will produce flowers. Like a flower, it will have many blooms. It will show its happiness, as if it were shouting with joy. It will be beautiful like the forest of Lebanon, as beautiful as the hill of Carmel and the Plain of Sharon. Everyone will see the glory of the Lord and the splendor of our God. Make the weak hands strong and the weak knees steady. Say to people who are frightened, "Be strong. Don't be afraid. Look, your God will come, and he will punish your enemies. He will make them pay for the wrongs they did, but he will save you." Then the blind people will see again, and the deaf will hear. Crippled people will jump like deer, and those who can't talk now will shout with joy. Water will flow in the desert, and streams will flow in the dry land. The burning desert will have pools of water, and the dry ground will have springs. Where wild dogs once lived, grass and water plants will grow. A road will be there; this highway will be called "The Road to Being Holy." Evil people will not be allowed to walk on that road; only good people will walk on it. No fools will go on it. No lions will be there, nor will dangerous animals be on that road. They will not be found there. That road will be for the people God saves; the people the Lord has freed will return there. They will enter Jerusalem with joy, and their happiness will last forever. Their gladness and joy will fill them completely, and sorrow and sadness will go far away.

Isaiah 35 NCV

The link—https://www.almanac.com/plant/lilies—will give you great information about our theme flower, help you buy the right bulbs to plant when you go to a nursery, and guide you through a step-by-step process of growing your lilies.

Day 8

A Time for Everything

The concept of time with words like "timing" and "timeless," along with phrases such as "appointed time" and "time is fleeting" are used constantly in our lives. These also ring out a bold and powerful message that God's timing in His plan is extremely valuable to His kingdom. For that reason, we must get rooted in the fact that the Lord does indeed have a purpose for our lives, so we need to seek out the meaning of time, according to the Bible's teaching.

Like faith, time cannot be held in one's hand. You are not able to reach out to hold even a minute. Yet time just keeps moving on. King Solomon wrote in Ecclesiastes 3:1: *"There is an appointed time for everything. And there is a time for every event under heaven."* He then launches into an intense list of extremes, beginning with *"A time to give birth and a time to die."* Proclaiming one event surely leads to another, he informs us that they all—good or bad—will happen under Heaven. Solomon reminds us that time will continue to move forward and so must we.

In Jesus' life, there was a time for everything—His birth to fulfill the prophecies, His first miracle, His teaching and healings. There was

timing in Him going to the Father in prayer, being alone, with the disciples, and the time to be turned over to the Pharisees. There was even a specific hour to carry the cross, to die, to be resurrected, and to take His place at the right hand of God.

We too need to move through the events of our lives that are also crucial to God's plan. You were chosen for the exact time in which you are living. Therefore, your life has purpose. You have been given numerous seasons to form extensive roots, grow and bloom to shine bright, pointing everyone you encounter to the truth that the *time* is at hand to seek the kingdom of God before all other things.

If we know that time is fleeting and the days are evil as the Bible clearly states again and again, then how must we thrive, not merely survive, during our lifetime? Not by pursuing earthly pleasures but rather seeking God's wisdom to live the best life with the amount of time we are given. Growing in relationships with our brothers and sisters. Being inspired by the creation we see in the heavens and the earth. Taking every moment captive to glean the wisdom to accomplish the will of God.

Jesus came into Galilee, preaching the gospel of God, and saying, "The time is fulfilled, and the kingdom of God is at hand; repent and believe in the gospel."

Mark 1:14-15

Roots

Why do you suppose growing deep spiritual roots that last takes so much dedicated and intentional time?

_____

_____

_____

_____

_____

Blooms

Why do you suppose our most beautiful and lasting blooms in life take the most time to nurture?

_____

_____

_____

_____

_____

Prayer

"Timeless One, You are Alpha and Omega, outside of our time and space. Thank You for every hour You have ordained for me to serve You. Empower and strengthen me to be the best steward of your precious gift of time. In Jesus' name, amen."

God placed you
right where you are
for such a time as this!

Day 9

AMONG THE THORNS

Some of the most beautiful flowers, both petite and hearty in size, and so fragrant grow alongside the lilies of the field. But there are also many wildflowers that are covered in thorns. As God's lilies in our culture, we too will find ourselves taking root, growing, and blooming right next to wildflowers. Beautiful, yes, but covered with thorns.

When we give our lives to the Lord, He plants us where He needs us. He then sets us apart, feeds, waters, and prunes, readying us to bloom in season. The preparation process we must go through might not look as appealing as the rapidly growing, thorny flowers that spread like wildfire all around. But God wants you strong, right where He has placed you, not being caught up in or overtaken by the thorns of this world.

Our eyes can become beguiled, so one can easily lose perspective by desiring to look like another. Our just and divine Savior knew this about His creation, empowered us through His Spirit, and informed us through His Scripture to keep our eyes on Him. Not to turn to the right or left, not to look around and yearn to have another's life, or wish to be elevated, admired, and praised.

As we grow and mature in Christ, we can learn to not be overtaken by thorns, but rather look at them as a place of growth. Seeing them for what they are and learning to dodge the sharp spines of the unruly plants of this world. Too often we judge the outer appearance before we understand why someone has been created as they are in the first place. In fact, we may even get angry and hostile towards what appears to be prickly and harmful to us, simply because we lack knowledge and understanding. But once we grasp the truth behind the thistles, we can then navigate our own growth in the field, no matter how many thorns.

God wants us to understand the grasp that thorns can have on His lilies. He wants us to learn, grow, and use every bit of wisdom and knowledge He has provided for us within the Bible to use to our advantage. Thorns may look alluring, pulling us in, and enticing us to pursue earthly pleasures, the approval of people, and unsatisfying relationships, but He wants us to see how we have been set apart and chosen by Him.

You can give glory to His name, shining bright as the marvelous eye-catching lily you are, not to look like the world or anyone else, but rather to stand high among the thorns for all to see. Always remember that you are uniquely created and were never intended to become anything other than the masterpiece that God fashioned you to be.

"Like a lily among the thorns,
So is my darling among the maidens."

Song of Solomon 2:2

Roots

What are some practical ways you can keep a healthy perspective that God has set you apart among the thorns of this world?

_____

_____

_____

_____

_____

Blooms

How might accepting and embracing your place as a unique lily of the field that must live among thorns actually accelerate your spiritual and emotional growth?

_____

_____

_____

_____

Prayer

"Great Redeemer, thank You that You see me as a beautiful and fragrant flower You have placed in this life for a plan and a purpose. Help me to grow stronger in my identity as a lily who cannot live as a thorn, but must love every wildflower in the field by Your grace. In Jesus' name, amen."

Beauty is
as beauty does.

BATHED IN BEAUTY

The book of Esther tells the powerful story of drama and romance about a young girl who would become a queen and saves her people from genocide. Full of intrigue, her story weaves together God's perfect timing, His sovereignty, and the choices humanity makes for good and evil. Esther also offers us a unique glimpse into the perpetual process of beautification completed by the Creator to glorify His kingdom and serve His people.

I will never forget the first time I read Esther. I felt empowered to know a woman like her was chosen by God, found favor in His eyes, and was called by Him to intervene for His children. She was not from a noble family of wealth and power, but rather a Jewish orphan raised by Mordecai, a family member. But that contrast is exactly what makes this story so relatable to us as women. Every time I read this marvelous story, I find new nuggets of unearthed gold to propel me forward in times of struggle and confusion.

All the women taken into the palace by the king's overseers were pleasing to the eye. Otherwise, they would have been left behind. But from a front-row seat, we quickly realize that the natural beauty of the women was only the beginning. According to their customs, there was a twelve-month beautification process that would enhance their every attribute, transforming a young woman into the potential to become queen.

Esther found favor with Hegai, a eunuch that served the king who navigated her personal makeover by providing the right caretakers, posh living quarters, proper diet, and finest cosmetics to give her the best opportunity at finding love and favor with King Xerxes.

The story of Esther reminds us that we too have been chosen to be a queen. Our Father takes each one of us through a beautification process to enhance our inner and exterior attractiveness. Just like the lily, planting, feeding, and providing us with the right elements of care. He bathes us in His beauty, exuding the love of Christ from our hearts and souls to find favor with those we meet, supplementing and shining bright from the inside out.

As Esther was uprooted from her home as a young girl and ushered off to live in a harem, no matter what she went through, she took root to trust and have faith that God had a plan for her life. Just as He does for you. Because of her deep roots, she was able to stand for her people against the schemes of evil, not because of her might, but because of the preparation she had undergone. As you become rooted in the Lord, you too will be bathed in His beauty.

*"Yet who knows whether you have come
to the kingdom for such a time as this?"*

Esther 4:14 NKJV

Like Esther, God has uniquely and purposefully placed you where you are, planted and rooted you in His kingdom, and blessed you with beauty "for such a time as this."

Roots

How has the deepening of your roots in Christ impacted your self-esteem and self-worth?

_____

_____

_____

_____

Blooms

How has your relationship with Jesus affected your countenance, your eyes, your face, your physical being, your inside displaying outwardly?

_____

_____

_____

Prayer

"Beautiful One, thank You that You view me as a queen and You have Your own beautification process that is radically different than the world's. Please make Your light shine inside out through every part of me. In Jesus' name, amen."

Nothing brightens
the countenance of your face
like Christ in your heart.

Day 11

THRIVE IN LIGHT

The Bible tells the story of God's purpose and plan for His creation, offering a roadmap, a blueprint for His children to follow. The first chapter of the book of Genesis chronicles the creation of the world and all living things that inhabit the planet. The words begin like a brushstroke of visual art across a blank canvas, empowering the reader to imagine the formation of the heavens and the earth. The Lord fills the skies, land, and water with creatures and vegetation of all kinds, ultimately forming man and woman in His image. Captivating and breathtaking in all its glory, God created our world and then placed us centerstage.

The Creator captivates us by all the incredible beauty, establishing us as both created *and* creative beings, preparing the landscape for us to see, believe, and engage. But for us to *see* His handiwork, we must first have light. Scripture states that He loomed over the dark abyss and said, *"Let there be light,"* thereby illuminating the landscape.

Throughout Scripture, light is often used to signify the Lord in His holiness, His power, and His goodness. His overcoming of the world. Life over death. Good against evil. God versus Satan. The Lord is the first and the last. He *is* light!

Without light, nothing in the world would be able to survive, let alone sustain ongoing life. So, we know that light is a necessary resource for all the plants, fish, animals, and human beings that God made. The Lord's work is genius, because not only did He start with light to begin creation, and then use light to reference Himself throughout the Bible, but He also uses light to support life. Because He *is* light, we are powered and sustained by Him.

We are created to thrive in the light for all our mental, physical, and spiritual needs. Even the sun is symbolic of God in so many ways, giving us warmth when we are cold, along with providing essential vitamins, serotonin, and melatonin. All extremely important to our wellbeing, providing nutrients for our bones, teeth, muscles, brain, and overall health. So we can see that God thought of every detail for today and eternal life.

When we give our lives to Christ and begin to grow in His Word, He can radiate just like light through us to everyone we encounter. We no longer walk in the darkness of this world, because through Christ's sacrifice, He exchanged it for His light. This very day, He lights our path. We must bask in the Son to grow, flourish, and thrive while we walk out our days in Him and for Him.

The Word gave life to everything that was created,
and his life brought light to everyone.
The light shines in the darkness,
and the darkness can never extinguish it.

John 1:4-5 NLT

So, shine bright, Sisters!

Roots

In what ways have you seen and sensed God's light in your life as you have grown in Him?

_____

_____

_____

_____

Blooms

How have you seen God's light emit from your life to shine to others as His witness?

_____

_____

_____

_____

Prayer

"Father of Lights, thank You for thinking of everything in such great detail to give us life. Thank You for physical light, spiritual light, and the ability to shine for You to light the way for others to follow You. In Jesus' name, amen."

Even on the darkest night,
the light from a single candle
can guide us home.

FRAGRANT AND FRUITFUL

I love lemons, so I asked our gardener to plant a well-developed and healthy lemon tree in the landscaping of our backyard. He found the perfect spot, giving it plenty of space to grow with lots of sunlight. Shortly after planting, the tree began to produce beautiful, hearty lemons. Seeing the brightly colored, fragrant, lush fruit, I began to dream about all the tasty treats I could make: an endless supply of tart lemon bars, lemon cakes, lemon spritzers, and so much more.

As I began gathering my first batch, I could see the tree was flourishing, the branches strong to hold the sizable fruit, allowing the best possible lemons to grow. The leaves were dark green and the skin of each lemon was waxy and fragrant. To the touch, they were heavy, assuring me that each fruit was full of juice and the rind optimal to use for all my culinary needs.

The Lord gave us all the incredible gift of our senses: sight, hearing, touch, taste, and smell. As Christ-followers, we have six, being given the additional sense of the Holy Spirit. Genius how the Lord created us with these powerful sensations to gather information about *anything* we encounter. In every environment, our physical senses can be

47

elevated to give us valuable and useful input. In every circumstance, the Holy Spirit can inform and instruct us in what God wants.

Jesus taught using parables to grant us knowledge of the mysteries of the kingdom of Heaven. He often used trees, branches, vines, and fruit as analogies in stories to tell us how to identify the walk of a believer by his or her spiritual maturity. Therefore, we must regularly stop and take inventory of our own lives to ask if we are producing His fruit. Questions like: Am I a healthy branch attached to Christ the Vine? Am I flourishing in a life surrendered to Jesus? Is my fruit multiplying to be everlasting? Just like my senses are used when I walk out to my lemon tree, we can use our senses to identify the fruit we are growing in our lives.

"Test yourselves to make sure you are solid in the faith. Don't drift along taking everything for granted. Give yourselves regular checkups. You need firsthand evidence, not mere hearsay, that Jesus Christ is in you. Test it out. If you fail the test, do something about it. . . . We're rooting for the truth to win out in you. We couldn't possibly do otherwise. We don't just put up with our limitations; we celebrate them, and then go on to celebrate every strength, every triumph of the truth in you. We pray hard that it will all come together in your lives."

2 Corinthians 13:5, 7-9 MSG

Sisters, let's agree to frequent fruit checks, shall we?

[For lots of good info on lemons and lemon treats, check out SaticoyLemon.com.]

Roots

Why do you think Paul would encourage us as believers to "test" ourselves? How might we benefit by checking our own fruit?

_____

_____

_____

_____

Blooms

What quality or spiritual fruit do you believe God has grown the most in your life that others enjoy and benefit from?

_____

_____

_____

_____

Prayer

"Master Gardener, thank You for my five physical senses and my sixth sense of the Holy Spirit. Guide me to use them all to experience You and test myself to be certain I am producing what You intend. In Jesus' name, amen."

Lord, help me
not to judge others,
but be a fruit inspector
of my own crop.

Overflowing With Fruit

Author Maya Angelou took a far more creative and tasty spin on the familiar lemons and lemonade colloquialism when she stated, "In all my work, I try to say, 'You may be given a load of sour lemons, so why not try to make a dozen lemon meringue pies?'" The first time I read that quote, I was reminded of my grandmother's award-winning pies. At least to our family, they were.

As a young girl, I would visit my grandmother often. Always upon my arrival, she had a delicious treat waiting. One of my favorites was her lemon meringue pie. I can picture it now: the tall meringue elegantly topping off the tangy yellow filling, giving visual beauty to the dessert as I would indulge in a slice of heavenly goodness. Every time, those tasty delights drew me in. As my fork would cut into the fluffy meringue and down through the filling, I imagined all the glorious fruit she gathered to make her masterpiece. Those warm, familiar memories of my grandmother always bring a smile to my face.

She may not have had much materially, but her wealth was in the ability to influence others with her love through her gift of baking. She would spend hours working away in her tiny kitchen to fill tummies

with a buttery, sugary treat. Then as they were consuming every bite as if it were their last, she would slip in some talk about the main ingredient in her own life—Jesus.

> *Open your mouth and taste,*
> *open your eyes and see—how good God is.*
> *Blessed are you who run to him.*

Psalm 34:8 MSG

God has created the tree that provides the branch for the lush lemon to grow, feeding and nurturing the fruit to be used in so many unique ways. My grandmother truly understood this truth and so must we. The Lord is doing the same through each one of us. He is the vine, and we are the branches. He provides us with life-giving food through His Word, empowering us to produce fruit in our lives, pointing all those we meet to "taste and see" the goodness of the ultimate Gardener. The end result is we will see lots of fruit overflowing from our lives when we are walking and growing according to His will.

Roots

As you have produced spiritual fruit, how has that experience encouraged you to mature and grow even more in Christ?

_____

_____

_____

_____

_____

_____

Blooms

What gift has God given you that naturally flows out from you to bless others?

_____

_____

_____

_____

_____

_____

Prayer

"Father, help me to keep discovering, growing, producing, and blessing others with the fruit You produce in my life. Empower me to also share the main ingredient in my life, to help others taste and see that You are good. In Jesus' name, amen."

Through a broken branch,
God can produce
fruit overflowing.

54

DIGGING DEEPER - TWO

In His World

Yesterday, I told you about my grandmother's lemon meringue pie, her gift of baking shared with her many guests, and her love for Jesus. I talked about how those all worked together in her rich life to impact and influence others.

Today, take your devotional time outside. Before you go, grab a piece of lemon meringue pie, a tall glass of lemonade, or some other fruity treat of your choice. Leave your phone inside. Just bring your book and your Bible. Find your favorite place to sit, take some deep breaths, relax, be still, and spend time enjoying a little taste of Heaven—literally. Allow some quiet time with just you and God with no distractions, while taking in His creation.

In His Worship

After you finish your treat and have slowed down a few minutes, take some time to seek the Lord and His will. Pray and ask Him to show you His unyielding fruit only He can create and provide. Focus on

His everlasting gifts in your life that are here with you today to bless others, will mature and grow through the seasons of your years, and then accompany you to Heaven. Write down any thoughts you have in your journal or the free space on these pages.

After you finish this time, read the passage provided below.

In His Word

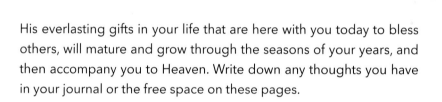

"And when you come before God, don't turn that into a theatrical production either. All these people making a regular show out of their prayers, hoping for stardom! Do you think God sits in a box seat?

"Here's what I want you to do: Find a quiet, secluded place so you won't be tempted to role-play before God. Just be there as simply and honestly as you can manage. The focus will shift from you to God, and you will begin to sense his grace.

"The world is full of so-called prayer warriors who are prayer-ignorant. They're full of formulas and programs and advice, peddling techniques for getting what you want from God. Don't fall for that nonsense. This is your Father you are dealing with, and he knows better than you what you need. With a God like this loving you, you can pray very simply. Like this:

Our Father in heaven,
Reveal who you are.
Set the world right;
Do what's best—
as above, so below.
Keep us alive with three square meals.
Keep us forgiven with you and forgiving others.
Keep us safe from ourselves and the Devil.
You're in charge!
You can do anything you want!
You're ablaze in beauty!
Yes. Yes. Yes.

Matthew 6:5-13 MSG

Prayer

Close today by praying Jesus' prayer. Make the words your own by changing "our" and "us" to "my" and "me."

Day 15

EXPERIENCING THE CREATOR'S GIFTS

Anytime I step outside, I am instantly pulled into the glorious fact that the Creator of the universe spoke into existence everything under the heavens and on the earth. He created all things to come into His presence and abide in Him. In Genesis chapter one, we see that the Lord has had a purposeful and well laid plan for our lives since the foundation of the world. From "let there be light" to "man should not be alone," God began with elements that best represent Him, creating us in His image, and then setting us apart from all other creation.

The knowledge of man and woman being formed in the likeness of God is greater than our human minds can ever comprehend. From cover to cover in the Bible, He wants us to know how important we are to Him. He informs us throughout the pages of our beauty, value, worth, and the fact that we are chosen.

Immediately, the book of Genesis identifies God as the Creator, Artist, Gardener, Master Planner, and Sculptor to give us a glimpse of His powerful imagination. Right away, He began to fill in the brilliant colors, unique shapes, and majestic creatures that would inhabit the world, setting in motion His plan to guide us during our time on Earth.

From engaging with creation through our five senses to experiencing His handiwork in creation to the gift of the Holy Spirit in us, God thought of everything. Clearly, He doesn't want us to miss out on knowing Him.

Sitting by the ocean, breathing in the salty air, listening to the great waves crash against the shore, or taking a hike in the middle of a lush forest, seeing the culmination of creatures and colors, or watching a baby grow from conception to birth, we are given the opportunity to experience the Force behind the beauty of creation. Whether we realize or not, we are constantly identifying and gathering information that points us to the Creator, the Master Planner.

But the basic reality of God is plain enough. Open your eyes and there it is! By taking a long and thoughtful look at what God has created, people have always been able to see what their eyes as such can't see: eternal power, for instance, and the mystery of his divine being.

Romans 1:20 MSG

Let us utilize all our senses, take in His creation, engage in His beauty, and embrace all of life to pursue the Creator who first pursued us.

Roots

How does creation provide personal evidence to you of God's plan and purpose for your life?

_____

_____

_____

_____

_____

_____

Blooms

What are some ways you express your belief to others that God is the Creator?

_____

_____

_____

_____

_____

_____

Prayer

"Heavenly Father, thank You that You allow us so many ways to experience You in this life and give us so much evidence of your life and love. Help me to continually see, hear, and feel 'the mystery of Your divine being.' In Jesus' name, amen."

While some say
they cannot see God,
I cannot not see Him.

MASTER GARDENER

We have all seen beautiful portraits and illustrations by famous artists who try to capture the essence of the Garden of Eden, known as "Paradise." They depict the Gardener's masterful design of the perfect environment for which all creation may dwell. These works of art invoke images and thoughts of the fresh air, rich untainted soil, crystal blue water, beautiful and unique animals, and humans made in His image—all undefiled with every element in its purest form sustaining life. Every animal and each person walked together throughout the garden in peace and harmony. Everything was perfect, living in an enormous, botanical utopia.

Genesis 2 tells us that God Himself planted multiple trees, plants, and flowers that danced with spectacular color, diverse in nature, filling the garden, all to fulfill His purpose. Some provided shade, some food, while still others vegetation, whether on the earth or in the ocean. Every species on land produced oxygen for living creatures and humans to breathe. Everything in the garden served a plan and provided the landscape for Paradise to exist. We too were created with a purpose to serve God and serve others. We are uniquely created to live together and produce where God has planted us.

As for me, I have always wished to have a "green thumb." But I'm sad to say that my planting and gardening skills are not very good. In fact, most plants I've tried to grow on my own, whether inside my home or in my yard, usually underperform. This is mostly due to my lack of knowledge on the proper care to be able to give them optimal growth. However, this is not at all true for the Gardener. Even though we do not live in the Garden of Eden, we do live in accordance with creation, and the Lord plants us where we will be fruitful to help nourish those we encounter.

The Garden of Eden illustrates living in harmony, where all of God's creation provides for the others to help any and all flourish and grow. That is why we must cooperate to take root, growing through His Word. Encountering the Gardener daily to bloom and bear fruit, giving off important elements to empower others to grow.

*If you've gotten anything at all out of following
Christ, if his love has made any difference in
your life, if being in a community of the Spirit
means anything to you, if you have a heart, if
you care—then do me a favor: Agree with each
other, love each other, be deep-spirited friends.*

Philippians 2:1-2 MSG

Roots

What has been your most difficult area of life to "take root" spiritually? Take a moment to write out why you think this may be hard for you.

_____

_____

_____

_____

_____

_____

_____

Blooms

What is one area where you desire to bloom, yet consistently struggle? Take a moment to write out why you think this may be hard for you.

_____

_____

_____

_____

_____

_____

_____

Prayer

"Heavenly Father, thank You that You didn't delegate creation to anyone, but You got down into the dirt with Your own hands. What an amazing thought. Help me to dig deep, to be okay with getting a little dirt on my hands for my best and Your glory. In Jesus' name, amen."

The same God who
plants, waters, and feeds
also trims, cuts, and prunes.

THE FATHER'S LOVE FOR HIS DAUGHTERS

Sometimes during my quiet moments alone in the morning, I imagine sitting at the feet of Jesus, looking up and seeing His face, full of love, kindness, and grace like I've never known before. I feel a love that only a perfect Father can give. The enduring nature that He has towards me, caring for me, meeting me right where I am, extending His hand to me, calling me His daughter. He wants to teach me His ways, to seek Him first for all my needs, trust in Him to care for me, and provide a purpose and plan for my life. He longs to hear my prayers, lending His powerful hand to guide my steps and navigate my life. God guides and directs us to see Him throughout the pages of Scripture and experience His Son, our Savior, in the Gospels.

He who has seen Me has seen the Father; how can you say, 'Show us the Father'? Do you not believe that I am in the Father, and the Father is in Me? The words that I say to you I do not speak on My own initiative, but the Father abiding in Me does His works. Believe Me that I am in the Father and the Father is in Me.

Jesus in John 14:9-11

When we see Jesus, we see the Father! The reality of His statement causes me to immediately respond in awe of the goodness of God. He would bring Jesus to the earth through a virgin, born in obscurity, to be given as the ultimate gift. The Savior of the world taking on human form to pursue us as only a Father would for His children. He thought of everything, giving us the best example in Christ.

Throughout the Gospels, we get an up-close and personal look at Christ's interactions with the disciples and all those He encountered, setting the stage for us to see the Father; One who has everything in control, schooling us in wisdom through parables, instructing us on His commandments to love Him and love others. Teaching us how to pray effectively, being fruit bearers, while giving us a powerful picture of Heaven. Informing us of the Father's love for us and the hope for our future.

Our Father wants the best for His girls. To see how Jesus interacted with the women in the Gospels is incredible. Tapping into the needs of women, Jesus stood as the Hero in front of the woman who was about to be stoned, the woman with the hemorrhage among the crowd of many, and sitting and talking with the woman at the well. All breathtaking and valuable moments, seeing His heart for His daughters and how important each one is to Him. With each encounter, He was preparing their hearts and minds to glorify the kingdom, just like He continues to do for us today.

As you read the stories of Jesus, see yourself in each of those women because He loves and cares just the same for you right now.

Roots

How do the stories of Jesus' interactions with women in the Gospels inspire and impact your relationship with Him?

_____

_____

_____

_____

_____

_____

Blooms

How would you describe God's love to appeal to the heart of another woman?

_____

_____

_____

_____

_____

_____

Prayer

For today's prayer, go back and read the first paragraph again and take a few minutes to imagine yourself sitting at the feet of Jesus. Say whatever comes into your heart to Him.

Remember, you will always
be a Daddy's girl
to your Heavenly Father.

Day 18

GOD LOVES UGLY

There are many mornings that I wake up not ready to take on the day. I lay in bed with my mind racing, feeling emotionally, physically, and spiritually bankrupt. Yes, much of the time it's my hormones, leaving me unmotivated to put my feet on the floor. Being honest, there are days I feel ugly, unruly, and unlovable. It takes everything inside me to get going, to fight off pulling the covers over my head and silently screaming.

As far back as I can remember, I have always dealt with female issues. Hormones that were either running too high or had completely dropped out of the race altogether, causing me to suffer, along with those who have had to live with me. Knowing this about myself helped me to better understand my needs, but I went through a lot of pain before I finally arrived at the knowledge and understanding of how to navigate my life. I knew there would be days of feeling hideous, even with a full face of makeup, hair perfectly curled, and a fabulous outfit to wrap up the package, masking the chaos that was going on inside.

Over the years, I have endured surgeries and medications through trial-and-error to find the right mental and physical balance for me to live a pain-free life. I suffered at the hands of doctors that, too often, actually made things worse. Many times over the years, I found myself on my knees, crying out to God for His help. And every time the Healer met me on the floor, rescuing me, giving me peace, and providing doctors that knew how to help. Today, I still go through a lot, but I can always count on the Father to see me in those moments and engage me in His loving-kindness.

In the process of writing this devotional, one day I found myself sitting on the sofa, struggling once again in one of *those* days. I started praying, tears streaming down my face, as I searched for the Lord through my confusion. I was reeling with false emotional, hormonal thoughts when He said to me, "Do you know how much I love you?" There I was, just like a little girl sitting on the lap of her Father, wrapped up in His arms when He continued, "Do you remember what John 3:16 says?" I answered out loud, "Of course I do." While my mind was spinning trying to recall the exact text, I opened my Bible and received God's love through His living words. There is something mystical and amazing about opening the Bible and receiving the power of the breath of God.

Sisters, I know that I'm not the only woman that goes through this emotional rollercoaster of ugly. But I do know that there is only One who can truly offer healing, peace, and unconditional love to inspire us to get up each day for Him, living our best possible life with the knowledge of the One who gave His life for ours. Your Father sees you as beautiful! So on those days, take inventory of your needs, make sure to seek His balance, and take them on with truth and great expectation.

"This is how much God loved the world: He gave his Son, his one and only Son. And this is why: so that no one need be destroyed; by believing in him, anyone can have a whole and lasting life. God didn't go to all the trouble of sending his Son merely to point an accusing finger, telling the world how bad it was. He came to help, to put the world right again.

John 3:16-17 MSG

Roots

Just as I shared, how has your faith helped you deal with your hormones and health as a woman?

_____

_____

_____

Blooms

How can you remind yourself the next time you feel ugly to quickly turn to your Father when those days come with their toxic thoughts?

_____

_____

_____

Prayer

"Heavenly Father, thank You that You love us at our ugliest. In fact, You offer me beautiful when I feel at my worst. On my ugly days, remind me and draw me to come straight to You for Your love, mercy, and grace. In Jesus' name, amen."

God always offers
His beauty
in exchange
for our ugly.

THE DOOR

I have been blessed to be able to travel over the years and visit many cities that are rich with extraordinary history and breathtaking architecture. Every time I see beautiful Victorian homes with their exquisite curb appeal, I fall in love all over again. I always think about the builder and the many details of the home's exterior and wonder how and why he or she made certain choices—colors, windows, the lush and vibrant landscaping that frames the home, ultimately leading the eye to the front door, always creating a visual masterpiece.

When my husband and I decided to update the exterior of our home, we consulted one of my dear friends who is an interior designer. She explained to us a simple goal she has, "To create the best first image someone sees when they arrive at your home, leading to a welcoming space for your guests." She always begins with the entryway. When you consider that as the first impression, the front door is truly a powerful image, adding the final exterior touch like a bow to a beautifully wrapped gift. From the interior, the door provides the warm glow of light, giving off a cozy feel that makes whoever enters sense they are home. But her explanation led me to dig into the history behind this hinged piece of art.

The first records offered of the door were in Egyptian paintings and were actually spiritual, representing the gate to the afterlife. In biblical times, doors were made out of wood, bronze, or stone. Some were adorned with symbols representing wealth, prestige, and reputation. Spanning thousands of years among multiple cultures, doors were used for different reasons. Some were merely to create ventilation, while others were used to signify occupants or workers' social status.

Here in the U.S., many colonial homes were actually built with a second front door, called the "coffin door" or "death door." The belief was when you were alive, you would enter through one door and when you passed away, you would come and go through "the death door." What a powerful image. Today, most people don't install their front door until the final stages of construction to add the finishing touch to their home.

Jesus is called many names in Scripture. The Door is one of those metaphors for Him. As a Christ-follower, we must identify Him as the door to new life and eternal life.

> *So Jesus said to them again, "Truly, truly, I say to you,*
> *I am the door of the sheep. All who came before Me*
> *are thieves and robbers, but the sheep did not hear*
> *them. I am the door; if anyone enters through Me, he*
> *will be saved, and will go in and out and find pasture.*
>
> John 10:7-9

Christ is the one Door that offers life after death. He has merged the life door and the death door into one. By choosing Him and going through Him, we are able to enter into the presence of God. What a beautiful image to see Jesus standing before us, guarding us from the enemy, while opening up life to allow us to walk into a new place and encounter the fulfillment of God's plan for our lives.

I'm so thankful we do not have to stand in front of multiple doors, being forced to choose which ones to walk through, that offer life or death, confusion or contentment, the enemy or the Lord. The Scriptures offer such clarity, giving us knowledge and wisdom to choose one door, the right door—Jesus.

Roots

What are some doors in your life you have faced, or walked through, that have shaped who you are today, whether helpful or harmful?

_____

_____

_____

Blooms

How has (or could) accepting that Jesus is your one Door to life affect how you perceive and decide upon all other doors you encounter in your life?

_____

_____

_____

Prayer

"Lord Jesus, the concept of the doors we face in life is a powerful metaphor. Please give me wisdom as I face my own choices to always see You as my Way, the Door to life, now and in eternity. In Your name, amen."

"Look! I stand at the door
and knock. If you hear
my voice and open the door,
I will come in, and we will share
a meal together as friends."

~Revelation 3:20 NLT~

Day 20

THE VOICE

We live in a fast-paced "I needed an answer yesterday" kind of world, don't we? When you stare at your phone, you can almost hear people saying, "Why aren't you answering my texts?!" Media is in our face all day long, every day. With a text tone or a notification beep, we have been conditioned to thrive in chaos. Whether we are watching TV, listening to the radio or a podcast, or scrolling social media, distractions come easily. Some of those are positive, giving us a much-needed shot of "you can do anything," while others are harmful, leaving us anxious and spinning out of control. I can often feel my blood pressure rising as my thoughts become fragmented. Living in this arcade kind of society has led me to become a firm believer in starting each day in a quiet space, focusing first on hearing from the Lord. So, take a deep breath and read on.

The crazy outcome of our world is that silence has become uneasy for many to deal with. As for me, I even need a "noise machine" at night because the volume of the quiet gives my brain too much room to work. I lie there and search back through my day, seeking answers to questions I encountered, making checklists for my kids, my husband, and yes, for me, too. Then I will move on to plan my best friend's birthday party in my head. Before I know it, I'm wide awake. So then I try to tackle world peace! That's when I roll over and attempt to drown out my inner voice and, all too often, the Lord's voice, too. Because of the noise, we often find ourselves looking for the Lord in the midst and mess of our lives, asking Him to speak, but sadly we are not in a position to hear Him.

One particular morning, I woke up, grabbed my coffee, and sat down ready to dig into my Bible. I kicked off my time with the Lord writing in my journal and thanking the Lord for another day. I sat there staring out the window, watching the sun come up as the light slowly illuminated the room. And then it hit me. I hadn't heard the voice of the Lord . . . for a while. I was listening. Or so I thought. I sat there for a few more minutes in that conviction and then I prayed, *Lord, I want to hear Your voice. Please speak to me and, when You do, please let me know it's You and not me just talking to myself.* Can you relate to this moment?

In His loving and faithful way, He led me to John 10 in my Bible. I was excited and expectant. I opened His Word and there He was: The Good Shepherd. As I began to read, the Lord reminded me that I am one of His sheep. I *will* know His voice. But I must seek Him and His ways so that I can discern His words and not be taken captive by the wolves of this world. Yet the only way that I'm able to hear and recognize His voice is by turning off the noise, silencing my thoughts, and listening for the One who gently whispers my name.

Truly, truly, I say to you, he who does not enter by the door into the fold of the sheep, but climbs up some other way, he is a thief and a robber. But he who enters by the door is a shepherd of the sheep. To him the doorkeeper opens, and the sheep hear his voice, and he calls his own sheep by name and leads them out. When he puts forth all his own, he goes ahead of them, and the sheep follow him because they know his voice.

John 10:1-4

Roots

Where is the loudest noise in your world coming from right now? Why is it so distracting?

_____

_____

_____

Blooms

How can you take a practical step to try and silence, or at least minimize, that noise and listen instead to the Good Shepherd—Jesus?

_____

_____

_____

Prayer

"Lord Jesus, help me to get to know Your voice so well that I can no longer hear the wolves and the thieves out to harm me. I want to listen when You call my name and obey every word You say. Help me to follow only You. In Your name, amen."

She that has ears to hear,
let her hear.

Day 21

DIGGING DEEPER - THREE

In His World

Can you hear Him whispering, "Come, sit with me"?

Yesterday, we discussed the never-ending noise and distractions of this world that can send us straight into the spin cycle. Today, I want to ask you to take your devotional time outside. Find a quiet place where you can sit, close your eyes, and play a calming instrumental song with no words, just a peaceful melody to soothe your soul. Silence your thoughts as you listen. I know this takes practice, but it's worth doing regularly for a few minutes. Invite the Lord into your day to speak to you. Listen for the voice of the Good Shepherd.

When you find your perfect spot, get comfortable, and take a few deep breaths. Pray and ask the Lord to quiet your mind. Ask Him to speak to you. Then listen intently for His voice. Turn on your music and begin to soak in your precious, powerful time with Him.

In His Worship

As your song comes to an end, thank Him for meeting you, sitting with you, pouring into you, and filling you up. Praise Him for being a Father who wants to be in relationship with you, growing you to glorify His kingdom. He wants to meet you right where you are, to defray your fragmented thoughts by hearing His voice in this noisy world.

In your journal or the margins of this page, write down anything that came into your spirit during this sweet time with the Lord. Allow the moment to become a reminder, encouraging you to grow in your walk with Him. Did He give you a Scripture? If so, turn to the passage in your Bible and write it down in your journal. Did He lay someone on your heart? If He did, note his/her name and the specific thoughts that came to you.

Allow your quiet time to empower your walk with Christ, as you make room to be shepherded by the One who comes looking for you every day, seeking you out, and bringing you back to Him. The more you tune out the world, the greater His voice will become. As you finish praying, read the passage provided below.

In His Word

"Rise up, my darling!
Come away with me, my fair one!
Look, the winter is past,
and the rains are over and gone.
The flowers are springing up,
the season of singing birds has come,
and the cooing of turtledoves fills the air.
The fig trees are forming young fruit,
and the fragrant grapevines are blossoming.
Rise up, my darling!
Come away with me, my fair one!"

Let me see your face;
let me hear your voice.
For your voice is pleasant,
and your face is lovely.

O my darling, lingering in the gardens,
your companions are fortunate to hear your voice.
Let me hear it, too!

Song of Solomon 2:10-14, 8:13 NLT

Prayer

As you close in a brief prayer, take in the powerful truth of how far, how wide, and how deep your Father's love is for you, how He wants to see your face, hear your voice, and how beautiful you are to Him.

Day 22

UNIQUELY CREATED

Thinking of ourselves as one-of-a-kind and uniquely created by God with a specific purpose and calling on our lives is often difficult for us to do. Yet the truth is that each one of us has been shaped and molded with specific gifts. It's up to us to seek out and hone in on what we have been given to glorify God and His kingdom. This may seem overwhelming, but to truly understand who we are and how we can influence others for Him, we must first understand *whose* we are and *who* we are. If the Creator of the universe fashioned us, then it's time to dig deep and get familiar with how He designed and defined each one of us.

Bible heroes like King David, Queen Esther, Joshua, Simon Peter, and Paul each had distinctive features, skills, and abilities that differed from the others. Just as they had to find their calling through God's Spirit, you too must seek out and identify what makes you uniquely you. First, you are a daughter of the King of Kings. Second, you are a bride designed and created for the Bridegroom. He has offered you the cup of life, and as you chose to accept it and receive the Holy Spirit living inside you now, He empowers you daily to be a world changer. *That truth should fire us up!*

Your DNA and fingerprints confirm you are uniquely created, including your specific personality traits, physical qualities, and natural talents. By becoming aware of and studying all you've been given, you can begin to align how they work together to optimize your God-given abilities to serve His kingdom.

Identifying your strengths and weaknesses is also crucial in this journey. We each have different approaches in handling tasks and people through our personalities. Maybe you are analytical, wise, and quiet or perhaps you are feisty, fast, and spontaneous. Maybe you are great at teaching children, but not very organized in your preparation. Some are musically inclined, while others are skilled in math. Maybe you are a great speaker or a strong runner. Once we start to recognize and establish potential talents, personality traits, strengths, weaknesses, and spiritual gifts, we are then able to hone in on the work we will have to do to become great at our gifts.

This journey often leads us to identify some hard truths about ourselves and the realization that we have to stop conforming to the idea that we can and should do *all* things. Instead, we can focus on how we can best serve God in His will. We are part of the body of Christ, and we must put in some personal work to see how and where we best fit. But always remember: you are one-of-a-kind, fused together with other believers to share the Gospel of Jesus.

For You formed my inward parts; You wove me in my mother's womb.
I will give thanks to You, for I am fearfully and wonderfully made;
Wonderful are Your works, And my soul knows it very well.

Psalm 139:13-14

Roots

What do you feel are your strongest anchors of who God has made you to be? The non-negotiables with which you know He has gifted you?

_____

_____

_____

_____

Blooms

What do you think your family and friends would say is your most visible weakness and your greatest strength? How do those actually work together for your good?

_____

_____

_____

_____

Prayer

"Lord Jesus, I want to discover every gift, trait, skill, and talent You have placed in me and maximize each one for Your glory. Please help me to be honest with myself about my strengths and weaknesses. I want to please You with all You have made me to be. In Jesus' name, amen."

This is your time, your season,
for God to empower you
in your unique design!

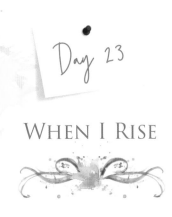

Day 23

WHEN I RISE

When I open my eyes each morning, my world starts moving quickly. I know that is true for most of us in this day and age. I always try to start by taking a deep breath and thanking the Lord for another day. Then I reach for my phone with the temptation always there to take a quick look at emails or social media. But I have realized that when I interact with the world before engaging with God, my behavior and passion tends to chase things instead of pursuing relationships. I can quickly find myself putting my own desires before the One who created me to be His passion, the One who continually pursues me.

Although we know that the world never stops spinning on its axis, somehow today it seems to move even faster. We are led to believe that if we don't engage with our most recent email, text message, or post on social media that we might miss out on something important. We could be ignored, disregarded, cancelled, or replaced by someone else. In fact, the acronym FOMO—fear of missing out— comes from this unhealthy way of living and has somehow been normalized, creating a strange anxiety and fear for far too many.

When we feel passionate about something, we will also develop a hunger that nothing else will satisfy. But misdirected passion can drive us to wrong actions, motivating us to pursue careers, relationships, and selfish dreams before we follow hard after the One who has created us and given us the passion in the first place.

Waking up every morning focused on gratifying our own desires pulls us farther away from peace and closer to chaos and confusion. Renewing our minds when we rise is critical to taking on our daily activities with spiritual eyes, listening ears, and receiving hearts that give way to pointing to the Lord first for our response to anything or anyone we encounter. When we passionately pursue Scripture, prayer, and worship, we are able to grow deep and hearty roots in our relationship with the Lord.

When we pursue Him first thing in the morning, gleaning His truth and power, we can't help but share it with those we meet throughout our day. That discipline helps us take our eyes off the world, as well as off ourselves.

As the beautiful lily that you are, I want to tell you once again that *you* have a divine purpose. And that purpose is Jesus. He desires that you follow passionately after Him, putting Him before all other things. So how about this? Let's have FOMO over not getting enough time with Jesus, rather than the world.

Sisters, let's shine bright, by putting on the full glow of the Lord when we rise in the morning.

But seek first His kingdom and His righteousness,
and all these things will be added to you.

Matthew 6:33

Roots

What is one practical step you can take today to place your focus on God and commit your day to Him first thing each morning?

_____

_____

_____

_____

Blooms

What is the main difference you see in the days where you are strong in the Lord versus the days where the world distracts you?

_____

_____

_____

_____

Prayer

"Lord Jesus, help me, lead me, to focus on You first thing in the morning before I do anything else. Remind me when I wake up that You are there, ready to show me what my life's direction should be for that day. In Jesus' name, amen."

When I rise,
may I keep my eyes
on the prize—Jesus.

THE PROMISED LAND

I will never forget one particular trip from Nashville, Tennessee to Norcross, Georgia, longing to hear the Lord's voice through a message as we were driving. I scrolled through different pastors' sermons, a women's conference teaching, and several podcasts, but nothing seemed to satisfy the hunger I had inside my soul. I thought maybe I just wasn't hearing what *I* wanted to hear. But then I remembered that one of my dear friends had sent a link to a message in a group text. The woman who was teaching was full of life and lots of fun to listen to. I was ready for whatever she had to say . . . that is, until she started to talk about Jericho.

No. Just no. . . . I wasn't going to listen to one more message about the walls of Jericho crashing to the ground after Joshua and the army marched, blew trumpets, and screamed their battle cry. Nope. Not today.

But as I reached to hit the power-off button, she began to share her testimony. Within a moment, I recognized her battle. She was up against the enemy trying to tell her lies, making her believe that she should turn back from the fight and stop trusting in the promises of

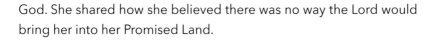

God. She shared how she believed there was no way the Lord would bring her into her Promised Land.

Her words struck my heart like a lightning bolt. Why? I, too, was stuck on the other side of the walls, walls that seemed too big to battle.

By the end of her story, she shared how the Lord had fulfilled the promise He had made to her in an even greater way than she could have ever imagined. The details of her testimony were undeniable and unmistakable and could have only been accomplished by the Father. That truth continued to echo in my spirit. Her message of Jericho and the Promised Land lingered with me for days—her beautiful testimony of not giving up the fight, while trying to believe God and His plan for her life.

Finally, I sat down and approached the Father, asking, *What are my walls?* After a few minutes in silence, He spoke and told me that I was in a battle of preparation. At first, I didn't get it as I thought about all my unanswered prayers. But then it hit me; preparation is a holy season that gives us the ability to seek the Lord, to trust in Him and walk by faith. That's when He takes us to the top of the mountain and shows us the impossible walls of Jericho to remind us, "You have already won. It's all yours." Then He gives us the command to fight.

> *Now Jericho was tightly shut because of the sons of Israel; no one went out and no one came in. The Lord said to Joshua, "See, I have given Jericho into your hand, with its king and the valiant warriors. You shall march around the city, all the men of war circling the city once. You shall do so for six days. Also seven priests shall carry seven trumpets of rams' horns before the ark; then on the seventh day you shall march around the city seven times, and the priests shall blow the trumpets. It shall be that when they make a long blast with the ram's horn, and when you hear the sound of the trumpet, all the people shall shout with a great shout; and the wall of the city will fall down flat, and the people will go up every man straight ahead."*

Joshua 6:1-5

Sisters, the walls of Jericho in our lives are very real and, for so many of us, they seem impenetrable. But let's not linger in the desert, but prepare ourselves to take them down and move forward. He wants us to be ready to share with the world how He was in the details of our lives, so that we can point to Him when we enter the Promised Land to take our territory for the kingdom of God.

Roots

What are the walls in your life that you feel have always kept you locked in or kept you locked out?

_____

_____

_____

_____

_____

_____

Blooms

What do you believe He wants you to do next to take the walls down that stop you from entering your own Promised Land?

_____

_____

_____

_____

_____

_____

Prayer

"Heavenly Father, I confess that the walls that create roadblocks for me are no problem for You. Give me the faith to believe You and trust that You can take them down for me. Help me to be proactive and march on while believing You have given me the victory. In Jesus' name, amen."

Shout! For the Lord
has given you the victory.

CEASE STRIVING

"Cease striving and know that I am God;
I will be exalted among the nations,
I will be exalted in the earth."

Psalm 46:10

There is freedom in the psalmist's quote from God for us to "cease striving." Sisters, I get it. Much easier said than done. But this is God's will for us, according to His Word. We are to literally rest in Him, in knowing Him, which means to find peace in His plan for our lives.

As a mother, wife, and professional, I don't get much time to rest; and when I do sit down for a few minutes or go to bed at night, many times, my mind continues to charge forward, checking off the lists, solving problems, and planning daily projects. The spin cycle seems endless, causing me a great deal of anxiety with lots of time to strive and little time to rest.

True rest—physical, mental, emotional, and spiritual—seems unattainable in the world we live in today. Whether we flip on the TV to catch the latest updates on the news or scroll through our social media feeds, many of us find ourselves viewing picture-perfect images of celebrities and "influencers," as we begin to play the comparison game. We often see the life of another woman and ask the pervasive question, "Why not *me*?" Striving to be perfect, successful, or famous can leave us lilies empty, spinning out of control and stagnating in our growth.

In those moments, I have to take some time to be still. I know those thoughts, those feelings, all too well of being jealous over another woman's life. A life that appears fruitful and filled with what I have been dreaming about. I know the "Why not *me*?" question well. But I refuse to stay in that place.

Lilies, we must stop striving and comparing ourselves to others, thinking that we are missing out on something that was never ours in the first place. Instead, we must thrive where the Lord has planted us by taking our eyes off the other beautiful flowers and keeping our eyes on the prize—Jesus.

One way we can cease striving and spinning is to deeply root ourselves in the Lord's Word to focus on *our* identity, talents, and gifts with which we have been uniquely created, for the time and place we are living in today. We have to see our lives as purposeful because of Jesus and our calling just as significant to change the world. Sadly, we have been sold a narrative that we must achieve a certain amount of success or followers to have a voice, to have a purpose that identifies more with titles than with the One who created us, the One who formed us in His image.

Today, as His lily, rest in the Lord and the plan He has for your life!

Roots

What are your most challenging places right now where you strive in your life?

_____

_____

_____

_____

Blooms

What one step can you take today to put your eyes on Jesus to rest in Him and His plan?

_____

_____

_____

_____

Prayer

"Heavenly Father, help me to focus on You more than myself, other women, social media, and what the world tells me I should look at and look like. Help me to turn the jealous 'Why not me?' moments into 'What can I do for You?' prayers. In Jesus' name, amen."

May I have the strength
to not strive,
the grace to thrive,
and the boldness
to live fully alive!

Day 26

DEALING WITH DISTRACTIONS

Asking a busy woman to disconnect from her fast-moving world first thing in the morning, or even for a period of time during the day, is a tough request, I know. As a wife, mother, and professional, I have to work to keep my eyes on Jesus in the morning and not get distracted. But for me to carve out time to be with the Father, I must get up in the morning and prioritize my devotional time. I need to receive His new mercies every morning to take on the day and all those I will encounter. If I look at my phone before my prayer time, I begin to make my lists. Head spinning, creating a to-do list for work while calendaring events, family needs, extended family events, vacation, grocery runs, dog grooming.

Sisters, you know the feeling. Our anxiety rises as we start creating lists in our minds, sending us into a total tailspin, and before we know it, we're on the hamster wheel of life, running the race as fast as we can even before our feet hit the floor in the morning. Once we take off on our daily race, then our prayers and time with the Lord often sound more like SOS calls than an "I need to hear Your voice" request. In the hustle of the day, we may find ourselves scrolling social media, adding to our level of stress, costing us time, health, and money.

We have to make sure that we have not overcommitted so we don't underperform.

Think about what distractions are costing you. How have they thrown you off course in the calling you desire to share with the world? Getting the education or training you need for the career God has called you to take on? Take a deep breath and realize that the Lord knows how the enemy is trying to distract you. Your Father wants to remind you, "Let nothing get in your way!" Or better yet, "Let nothing get in My way of what I have in store for you!"

When we're taking on something big for God, prioritizing our tasks is so important—lest we pursue so many things that we run out of energy and find ourselves confused, questioning God and His plan for our lives. Yet amidst all the demands and distractions, we can choose Jesus every single time. We must keep our eyes on the prize by kicking off every morning with the One who created us. Just like the lily, we were each created to flourish, not toil and spin out of control, worrying about tomorrow or being distracted by the temptations and worries of this world.

The faithful love of the Lord never ends!
His mercies never cease.
Great is his faithfulness;
his mercies begin afresh each morning.

Lamentations 3:22-23 NLT

Roots

What is the biggest distraction in your life right now that tends to keep you from spending consistent time with God?

Blooms

If you have struggled with staying on track with these readings, what practical step or steps could you take to make this a daily priority to finish strong?

_____

_____

_____

Prayer

"Heavenly Father, one of the best ways to rid myself of the distractions of life is to realize You should be my number one attraction. Help me to see that my time with You should never be a religious exercise, but more like a date with my Dad. In Jesus' name, amen."

The enemy's attractions
are disguised distractions
that can become
costly transactions.

PRAYER WARRIORS

There have been many times in my life when I've felt like I cannot keep pushing the boulder up the mountain. Too often, when I finally get close to the top, I give out and the rock rolls back down over me! My spirit is crushed, leaving me weaker than ever, unable to keep going. But when I find myself in that place, the Lord reminds me of *the Women in my World*. Sisters who come alongside me to simply listen to my disappointments, yet when I'm done, lead the way by offering, "Can I pray for you?" With a sweet but gentle nudge, they remind me that I have access to our Father. Women empowering women with the power of prayer.

One of the greatest gifts we've been given is the ability to communicate with our Father in Heaven, establishing a deep relationship with the One who created us. As He pours into us, we are then able to pour into others, encouraging them to pray, too. In doing so, we have the ability to move mountains and change lives for the kingdom of God. Sisters, we need other women to help lift up our heads and remind us to keep our eyes on Jesus. Sharpening us to tap into the Holy Spirit for direction and answers.

*Before daybreak the next morning, Jesus got
up and went out to an isolated place to pray.*

Mark 1:35 NLT

Jesus was our greatest example of seeking the Father first before
looking to the disciples or the world. But He also illustrates to us that
there is power in numbers by gathering together His twelve to do life
and ministry. They were His trusted friends. His desire was that they too
would become prayer warriors, seeking wisdom and understanding
to withstand every attack, meet every need, and enact every miracle
to fight on their knees for Him and those they would shepherd. We
too must follow in the footsteps of Jesus where the power to do all
things comes from.

> *"Again I say to you, that if two of you agree on earth about
> anything that they may ask, it shall be done for them by
> My Father who is in heaven. For where two or three have
> gathered together in My name, I am there in their midst."*

Matthew 18:19-21

The Women in my World empower me through prayer, pointing me
to seek truth in Scripture to propel me forward, reminding me we are
like the lilies that form colonies, great in number in our blooms, and
underneath the soil, growing intertwined, deep roots.

Sisters, I know this is easier said than done, but let's rally our troops, the other women in our lives that we know will put on the armor of God for us all to do battle on our knees until the war is won. When the boulder has rolled over you, the prayer warriors in your life will rescue and push you to keep your eyes on Jesus, allowing for healing and growth.

Roots

How has prayer made you stronger spiritually, emotionally, and mentally?

_____

_____

_____

Blooms

What are some practical ways you can connect with other women to pray for one another?

_____

_____

_____

Prayer

"Lord Jesus, if You needed time alone with the Father, then I certainly do. Lead me to my 'two or three to gather in Your name' to pray as sisters, standing strong in You for one another. In Your name, amen."

Lift your head,
eyes on Jesus,
armor up!

112

Day 28

Digging Deeper - FOUR

In His World

Armor up, women warriors of God!

Yesterday, we rolled back the rock revealing the highs of standing on top of the mountain and the lows of lingering in the valley. We were reminded that our God is the light in dark places. He is the God of relationship and, in turn, has created us to be in relationship with others, to encourage and inspire, and most importantly, pray for one another.

Today, I want to encourage you to take the time to call one of your sisters in Christ and invite her to join you for a time of devotion at your favorite coffee shop. Come together and begin by talking about what the Lord has done for you since you last saw one another. Praise Him for what He is doing in your life. Then both of you share your prayer requests.

Consider making this a regular prayer time with your sister (or sisters), committing to pray for each other daily to watch what God does.

Face-to-face time with other women is so important to help us grow as warriors of God, to empower us to walk in our seasons of life in strength, confidence, and beauty.

Whether we are broken or jumping for joy, Sisters, we must meet and pray for one another.

In His Worship

"Iron sharpening iron" from Proverbs 27:17 is one of my favorite visuals of believers coming alongside one another. Each strike of the blade against the other makes both effective and ready to use. No matter how sharp or dull either blade was at the beginning, the intentional friction will make each better, more useful, and ready to fulfill its purpose.

During your time together, offer one another godly advice, constructive criticism in truth and love, always seeking the Lord first. Remember the importance of trust, accountability, and transparency as you open up your conversation and watch the sparks fly!

Next, read the passage provided below where Paul speaks of the spiritual battle and how our only hope to win in this life is through Christ and working together.

In His Word

And that about wraps it up. God is strong, and he wants you strong. So take everything the Master has set out for you, well-made weapons of the best materials. And put them to use so you will be able to stand up to everything the Devil throws your way. This is no weekend war that we'll walk away from and forget about in a couple of hours. This is for keeps, a life-or-death fight to the finish against the Devil and all his angels. Be prepared. You're up against far more than you can handle on your own. Take all the help you can get, every weapon God has issued, so that when it's all over but the shouting you'll still be on your feet. Truth, righteousness, peace, faith, and salvation are more than words. Learn how to apply them. You'll need them throughout your life. God's Word is an indispensable weapon. In the same way, prayer is essential in this ongoing warfare. Pray hard and long. Pray for your brothers and sisters. Keep your eyes open. Keep each other's spirits up so that no one falls behind or drops out.

Ephesians 6:10-18 MSG

As we close today, consider these questions:

- Who are you fighting the good fight alongside?
- Who is making you strong and who are you making strong?
- Who do you need to make sure doesn't "fall behind or drop out"?

THE POTTER

I have a sweet friend who recently purchased a pottery wheel. She posts breathtaking pictures of her process on social media, telling the story of each unique piece she brings to life, using her imagination to form the lifeless lump of clay. As I scroll through her photos with great anticipation to see her latest masterpiece, I can't help but notice the intimate details she creates with each image.

She sits down in front of her simple machine, places the block of greyish-color clay in the center of what looks like a metal plate. A small bowl of water, a soft, manageable sponge and a scoring tool sit next to her. She gently presses the peddle, setting the wheel in motion, as the clay waits for the potter's hands to begin.

Soon, as both hands are covered in clay and water, her dominant hand begins to form the piece of art while the other gently presses the soft, damp sponge to the creation, guiding it along the outer edges. She then picks up the scoring tool, cutting away what she doesn't need, as she streamlines the piece of clay moving on the wheel, making any last adjustments, adding to her design. Finally, in the closing picture, I can see the joy on her face as she holds her new creation in her hands.

But now, O Lord, You are our Father,
We are the clay, and You our potter;
And all of us are the work of Your hand.

Isaiah 64:8

I imagine God the Potter holding each one of us, looking at His work of art with love and adoration. This illustration gives us a powerful picture of the creation of man, with the Potter sitting down at His wheel, placing dust onto the center, gently pressing down the pedal to begin the movement as He begins to work the unformed material, sculpting, and cutting away anything unnecessary. He sees that His creation is beautiful, leaning over to breathe life into the man. Soon after, the Potter creates the woman. This time, forming her beauty from the bone of man.

Sisters, you are created and formed from one of the strongest materials on Earth. The Potter fashioned us out of bone as the helper to man. He created us with a unique DNA, formulating our strengths, weaknesses, temperaments, talents, and gifts. He purposed us as only the Potter could, knowing that man and woman together would be one of the most significant vessels He would create. You are an *original* work of art, God's masterpiece!

Throughout Scripture, the Lord uses stories, casting Himself in different roles, in various professions, establishing the skills and importance of each one—the Potter, the Gardener, the Shepherd, the Master Planner, all in accordance with the life journey we have with the One who created us. We are the pottery He holds in His hands, to use wherever He places us.

Roots

How can your ever-increasing understanding that God uniquely and intentionally created you affect your self-image and self-esteem?

_____

_____

_____

_____

Blooms

What is one feature, gift, talent, or skill that you have seen God use for Him lately?

_____

_____

_____

_____

Prayer

"God, forgive me when I allow myself to get hardened and unusable. Help me to stay soft and pliable, so You can always create what You want with my life and do with me as You please. In Jesus' name, amen."

I submit to Your shaping,
to the molding of Your hand,
to know You as the Potter,
my purpose to understand.

YOUR PURPOSE

Purpose is a big topic to tackle for any of us. But the one lens of truth through which we must see that purpose is Jesus. When I'm speaking with women, whether one on one or in a group setting, I will ask them to raise their hands if they know their purpose. The response is usually a mix of answers, but I find more often than not, women of all ages are still trying to figure this out. From all walks of life, we question ourselves, wondering if we have "the right answer." Nothing can leave us as confused as misunderstanding or not knowing our purpose.

The world today sells us a narrative that finding our purpose is always a journey, never a destination. Whether that be in our families, careers, ministries, or whatever we are longing for in the moment. Whether that be a dream, passion, or desire of our hearts that fits what we believe to be our purpose. But what happens when our kids go off to school? Or, God forbid, our husband passes away? Or our marriage comes to an end? Or we don't get the job we desperately prayed about for months? These events and other circumstances like them are seasons in life, not our purpose. This is exactly why the subject of purpose is so important for us to be confident in our identity and who the Lord is in our lives. We must find our purpose, not in anyone or anything other than Christ.

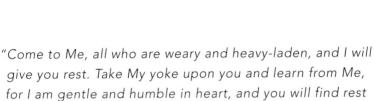

"Come to Me, all who are weary and heavy-laden, and I will give you rest. Take My yoke upon you and learn from Me, for I am gentle and humble in heart, and you will find rest for your souls. For My yoke is easy and My burden is light."

Matthew 11:28-30

If Jesus' words are true, then why would our Savior keep us running from one thing to the next trying to find our purpose? He wants us to live in freedom by coming to Him. Christ lived a life devoted to the Father and everyone He encountered. His purpose was to share the good news of salvation while always pointing towards and glorifying the Father. He lived according to the Father's will all the way to the cross.

You were created to serve Him and the kingdom of God, while also serving others with your life. Once we can understand that our purpose is secure in our Lord, then we can begin to walk in freedom, and also into our calling to use our talents and gifts that He has given us.

Sisters, let's rejoice as we look to the words of Jesus where we find rest for our weariness, an easy yoke, and a burden that is light. All you beautiful lilies, take heart and know that the Lord wants you to walk in freedom, knowing your purpose is secure in Him.

Roots

How could securing your purpose in Christ help you navigate the seasons of your life, whether triumphs or tragedies?

_____

_____

_____

_____

Blooms

Is there anyone, anything, or any circumstance that you feel gets in the way of defining your purpose in Christ? Why?

_____

_____

_____

_____

Prayer

"Lord Jesus, help me to clear away the distractions that keep me from Your purpose. I desire to be Yours first before I belong to anyone or anything else. Help me to learn from You and find rest for my soul. In Jesus' name, amen."

Accepting God's purpose
must come before we can
access God's plan.

LET'S BE REAL

I often talk with the Women in my World about having real relationships. We all agree that two of the main ingredients we look for are transparency and authenticity. In essence, to be allowed to see into each other's hearts, but then finding that what you each experience is real. The women who are a part of my colony have all shared the importance of deep, rich, meaningful connections with other women and how that dynamic is significant to emotional and spiritual growth. Those relationships influence all our lives by sharing truths about daily struggles, finding peace, and constant reliance on the Lord, allowing us to know we are not alone in life.

These emboldened conversations lead us to talk about the ways that we enter into relationships in today's culture. Many share how social media friends and influencers inspire them, impacting their daily walks by offering profound and intimate messages on their platforms, encouraging followers to engage in dialogue, giving them a sense of commonality, relatability, and vulnerability that we all long for. While there's nothing inherently wrong with these connections, they can leave us void of true human connection. We must remind ourselves to spend more time looking other women in the eye than being on our phones.

Yet the allure of online relationships is very real. We can be inspired there and even feel that it's easier to engage with people we *don't* know, revealing truths about ourselves inside a large and often anonymous community. As our culture becomes more and more dependent on the online experience, we too find ourselves relying upon a virtual friend to encourage us, rather than an actual human being. But sharing our feelings with hundreds of strangers can leave us empty when there is no response or affirmation of our personal worth.

Our communication skills today are being dulled down and, in too many cases, even lost. Engaging in one-on-one conversations is challenging for many today. And, unfortunately, this behavior has affected the way we spend time with the Lord as well—how we communicate with Him in prayer and wait to hear His voice. Let's remind ourselves that He desires to meet with us, to pour into us so that we can then in turn pour into others.

So Sisters, let's remember that we were created for relationship by the God who offers the ultimate friendship. Because Jesus was the Creator of interaction, we too desire the same for growth, companionship, friendship, and relationship. We have the need to share our inner thoughts on important topics with others. We yearn to be heard and be seen. And yes, to be challenged and corrected, even when it doesn't feel good. Throughout Scripture, Jesus repeatedly looked people directly in the eye and spoke to them with love, creating a genuine bond. He empowered those He encountered to feel valued, worthy, and important. And isn't that what we are all longing for?

Let us hold tightly without wavering to the hope we affirm, for God can be trusted to keep his promise. Let us think of ways to motivate one another to acts of love and good works. And let us not neglect our meeting together, as some people do, but encourage one another, especially now that the day of his return is drawing near.

Hebrews 10:23-25 NLT

Roots

How do you think being online and any dependence on that experience has affected your relationship with God?

_____

_____

Blooms

What practical step can you take this week to decrease your online activity and increase your face-to-face relationships with other women?

_____

_____

Prayer

"Heavenly Father, the internet is such an amazing resource, yet that is all that it is. A screen can never replace You or the people in my life. Please help me to balance my time online with growing in my personal relationships—first with You and then with others. Help me to be real in all things in my life. In Jesus' name, amen."

Which would your family and friends say you have more of a relationship with —your phone or your Father?

Day 32

THE GIFT

For years, one of my ministries has been to speak at Christian events. One of my greatest passions and privileges is when I am invited to share my testimony and offer a challenge at fundraising events for pregnancy care centers. I'm always honored to be a part of such beautiful life-preserving gatherings.

One such time was for the annual gala held by Blue Ridge Pregnancy Care Center in Lynchburg, Virginia. Because my purpose in being invited to speak is to help raise awareness as well as funds, I always like to tour the host's facilities prior to the event. I want to gather information about the center, understand their needs, and the best part, meet their team. These visits always inspire and move me to see how many men and women have obediently become the hands and feet of Jesus, serving others in the hope that they choose life— both theirs and their baby's—all while providing free support and resources. These events are always such a gift to my life and faith.

The last stop for this particular tour was the offices for the staff and volunteers. One of the leaders opened a cabinet door to reveal shelves stacked with Bibles. The young woman took one out and began to show me how each one was highlighted with custom tabs, pointing to special verses that adorn the pages and guide the reader. Every woman that comes through the center's door is given one of these masterpieces.

As the woman closed the cover, she handed it to me and said, "Shari, we'd like you to have this Bible." In the moment, the Lord spoke to me and I blurted out, "Would each one of you please write your name and your favorite verse on the first page for me?" Gladly, each one signed it and wrote down the reference for their verse.

At that time in that particular season, I had been struggling with some difficult life circumstances and challenges. Little did I know that the Lord had a plan to use this gift in my own life. My response to hearing His voice and my request to those women would help me get back into His Word. To give me a gift of the Living Water I was thirsting for, to once again flourish and grow, even in adversity. Back at home, I began searching for each verse the ladies had written down for me, inspiring me to spend time with the Lord.

This was a powerful reminder that each one of us will encounter dormant and dark times in our lives. Though seasons bring change and uncertainty looms around every corner, we have been given the Living Word. Like the lilies, we were created by the Father who gives good gifts to His children. So, of course, He feeds us the right food, giving us nourishment according to our needs. No other gift has the ability to change our lives for eternity like the Word of God. Truly, the gift that keeps on giving. So, hold onto Scripture like your life depends on it. Because it does!

For this reason we also constantly thank God that when you received the word of God which you heard from us, you accepted it not as the word of mere men, but as what it really is, the word of God, which also is at work in you who believe.

1 Thessalonians 2:13

Roots

When has God's Word spoken hope to you during a time of crisis? Share.

_____

_____

_____

_____

Blooms

When have you had the opportunity to share a verse or passage with someone to offer them hope? Share.

_____

_____

_____

_____

Prayer

"Heavenly Father, thank You for the gift of Your Word. Thank You that Scripture does keep on giving throughout my life, speaking fresh and new truth into my heart, especially in times of crisis. Help me to stay hungry and thirsty for Your words in Your Word. In Jesus' name, amen."

God will never compromise
His Word for you,
but He will always
customize His Word to you.

Day 33

LEAVING A LEGACY OF LOVE

A dear friend of mine had agreed to meet me for lunch at a little restaurant in Sherman Oaks, California. Greeting one another with a long hug after a difficult season in life always feels so good, especially when we never know what tomorrow will bring. We sat down and dove right in to catch up, sharing the struggles of recent moves, raising boys, the new seasons of life we were both encountering, and our experiences of working in Hollywood. We both chuckled as we acknowledged our lengthy journey in the entertainment business. Especially as Christians, we have seen first-hand much of the conception of faith-based content.

As we continued to share, we couldn't help but delight in the fact that the Lord has brought so many of His men and women to Hollywood, placing them on the battlefield of "show business," with a good number finding success as well as platforms to share the message of Jesus, whether behind or in front of the camera. We rejoiced together in all the Lord has been doing, recognizing that He has allowed us to be a part of His beautiful plan as well.

The conversation brought back memories for us both, but it also spurred our hearts in how we work in an industry that seems to continually pull further away from anything Christian. As we continued discussing how we were using our talents and gifts to get the next job, we realized that it's really not about the jobs at all, but rather how we continue to run the race—how we ultimately leave a legacy that truly points people to Christ through our families, relationships with business colleagues, connections with acquaintances, and even those we will never meet that are touched by our work. But in the end, the art we create that shares the sweet message of a Savior who loves us and died on the cross for us, that is our legacy. Pointing the next generation to the Creator of the universe, to identify with Him to communicate that they too can create a legacy of a life well lived by faith, believing in the promises of the Lord.

Sisters, *what* we do today, as well as *how* we do it, will affect all our tomorrows, causing a ripple effect of reaching people for Christ. Our legacies should reflect our love for everyone in our circles of influence, but most of all, it should point everyone that has ever known us to undeniably say, "She loved and served Jesus first and, second, others before loving herself." Let our lives shine bright for Jesus, reflecting a radiance that can only come from the Master Planner of the universe.

So when you're ready to call it quits, when life's not looking the way you think it should, in whatever the Lord has called you to, just step out in faith, and run at it with all your might. Persevere, women of God! The imprint of your life will be left for others to see and receive from, empowering them to get to know Jesus, propelling them to desire to also leave a legacy as they make an impact on the world.

So let's not allow ourselves to get fatigued doing good. At the right time we will harvest a good crop if we don't give up, or quit. Right now, therefore, every time we get the chance, let us work for the benefit of all, starting with the people closest to us in the community of faith.

Galatians 6:9-10 MSG

Roots

Whose example and legacy have inspired you in your faith journey? Why did that person or persons make an impact on you?

_____

_____

_____

Blooms

Write down the names of the people you know are looking to you right now for inspiration in their faith? Who has God recently placed in your life that you want to impact?

_____

_____

_____

Prayer

"Lord Jesus, You left the ultimate legacy for us to follow. I know the way for me to create a path for others to follow will be found by walking closely with You. Help me to see all of my life and all my relationships through Your lens to create Your legacy in me. In Your name, amen."

Our legacy will not
be determined in the
years to come, but in
the moments we live today.

PRECIOUS TIME

There's nothing quite like sitting in silence listening to the "tick tock" of the hands of the clock, reminding us our time is passing. Constantly aware of that reality, we think of time, all the time! Merriam-Webster defines the concept as, "an appointed, fixed, or customary moment or hour for something to happen, begin, or end." Yet we cannot harness or stop time; it just keeps moving through our lives. Because of our faith, we have a unique perspective of the importance of time.

Time travel has been the subject of countless books and movies, focused on the significance of the hours of our days and how our lives influence others. Historical heroes and historic events pinpoint specific times that have impacted the world, saved lives, announced births, and memorialized deaths, especially those willing to die to save others. Moses and Queen Esther in the Old Testament and Mary and Paul in the New Testament are just a few that were ready and willing when the Lord called their names and appointed them for their time. I find great peace in reading their stories, giving me a better understanding and greater knowledge of how to apply their testimonies of growth, waiting, struggles, and faith for my own life and times.

As I grow in my relationship with Christ and others, I am able to see the significance of how time plays a much greater role in the overall plan of God and how all the pieces and His people must come together to point towards Him, making the impossible possible. As in the story of Moses, after being born, he was placed in a river and found by Pharaoh's daughter, raised as an Egyptian, ultimately leading the Hebrew people out of slavery and into a time of waiting. The intersection of people, places, and events all took place for God to get the glory through a relationship with His people.

When we're tackling something big for God, the enemy will try to distract us, stealing our time. So, Sisters, this is why we should hold fast, knowing that we must use our time wisely, growing deep roots, and preparing ourselves, so when our time to shine for Him comes, we too are ready. Our time is of the essence, making it even more important to start our days off with the Lord as He prepares us for all He is calling us to accomplish.

But as for me, I trust in You, Lord, I say, "You are my God."
My times are in Your hand; Rescue me from the hand of
my enemies and from those who persecute me. Make Your
face shine upon Your servant; Save me in Your faithfulness.
Let me not be put to shame, Lord, for I call upon You.

Psalm 31:14-17

Roots

Describe the most impactful personal time you have ever had with God.

_____

_____

_____

Blooms

What event or circumstance has been the highlight of your walk with God in experiencing His work through you for the sake of others? Share.

_____

_____

_____

Prayer

"Heavenly Father, when I think of the seasons of my life and the time I have spent with You, one thing I know for certain is that I want the rest of my days to count even more, as I serve You in deeper ways and get closer to You. My time is Your time. My days are Your days. In Jesus' name, amen."

Time is not an inheritance
to be spent,
but an investment
to be shared.

DIGGING DEEPER - FIVE

In His World

God created time and throughout the Bible we see its importance.

Yesterday, we discussed the significance of our appointed moments in God's precious time. We witnessed through our heroes in Scripture those who were empowered by God and perfected in His timing to glorify His kingdom.

Today, during your devotional time, let's dig deeper as I introduce a concept that I call "mapping." This exercise will help you identify people and events in your life as well as your time. You will be able to see how the Lord is intersecting time to grow your world and gain a better picture of the spiritual race you are running.

Often, we can feel as though we are dormant, stagnant, and have not moved. But when we begin to put facts, not feelings, down on paper, our perspective can change. We can see with our own eyes how the Lord is bringing all things together. So, let's get started!

Grab your journal or a large piece of paper and a pencil. A pencil with an eraser, trust me, you might need it. First, draw a bullseye. Then draw some concentric circles around the bull's-eye, just like an archery target. In the center, write "Jesus" and then your name next to His.

In His Worship

Next, as you sit with the Lord, pray and ask for His help. Let Him be your Cartographer. Inside your circles, write down the name of anyone that comes to mind as a key relationship. Place their name in relation to how close they are to you. For example, a best friend is just outside you and Jesus, while a new acquaintance might be in the outer circle.

With each person, think about the relationship and the journey that created the connection. Watch for the "relational flow charts" of how one person may have introduced you to several others on your list. Keep listening for names, writing them down, and connecting the dots of what God has done and brought about in your life through others.

Once you feel like you are done, take a look at the timing of each encounter and begin thanking God for each person. Pray for him/her. Identifying the relationships and connections in your life can be very helpful to see the map of your life in real time as you set in motion a fresh vision for your calling, a new season, or dream.

Meeting others is a divine appointment and how you manage those relationships will be up to you. All with you and Jesus right there together in the middle of the bullseye.

In His Word

And then God answered: "Write this.
Write what you see.
Write it out in big block letters
so that it can be read on the run.
This vision-message is a witness
pointing to what's coming.
It aches for the coming—it can hardly wait!
And it doesn't lie.
If it seems slow in coming, wait.
It's on its way. It will come right on time.

Habakkuk 2:2-3 MSG

Keep your map with your Bible and use it as a reminder and prayer guide. Occasionally, you might want to start over and write a new one as you evaluate and reevaluate God's plan for your relationships, or be sure to continually add any new names that come into your life.

BEAUTIFULLY FLAWED

In 2011, I had the privilege of being cast in the film *October Baby,* an experience that changed not only my life but the lives of many others. One of my favorite lines from the movie is, "Life's journey is beautifully flawed." I continue to experience this truth daily, constantly reminding me that life is made up of seasons, peaks and valleys, floods and deserts. Like the lily, those seasons determine our growth as we bloom and develop, a robust flower, springing forth beauty.

I often encounter women struggling with their past, living in shame and holding onto dark secrets as the enemy works to hold them back from shining bright for Jesus. Instead of walking in freedom and believing that He has a plan for each and every life, our past can shut us down, thinking that we've lost our purpose and we aren't "good enough." That we have somehow missed the mark by committing something unforgivable. We then respond by declaring, "I can't possibly shine for Jesus."

But the answer to that false belief is that His glory must be magnified through our stories. Despite our personal tragedies, finding healing and redemption through our faith in Jesus Christ is possible, because He died on the cross for *all* our flaws—past, present, and future. We have to flip the script to say, "If I know Jesus and He lives inside of me, how could I not shine when He is the light of the world?"

> ". . . You're here to be light, bringing out the God-colors
> in the world. God is not a secret to be kept. We're going
> public with this, as public as a city on a hill. If I make you
> light-bearers, you don't think I'm going to hide you under a
> bucket, do you? I'm putting you on a light stand. Now that
> I've put you there on a hilltop, on a light stand—shine! "

Matthew 5:14-16 MSG

The more I grow in my walk with Christ, the more I see how He desires to use *all* of me, *all* of my life. This knowledge hasn't always been easy to grasp, to share my dark secrets with others, friends or strangers. But I have seen the fruit from the obedience of sharing my testimony through the many seasons of my life. Today, as I look back on my past, I realize God was always preparing me for my future.

Sisters, if He has a calling on my life, then He has a calling on yours, too. And He wants *all* of you! He wants you to share your story of His redemption, shining His Light. Jesus loves you just like He loved all those in the Bible. He wants you to be released from the enemy to find freedom to blossom while spreading seeds for others to grow. As believers, we are empowered by those He chooses to use, and I find confidence every day in knowing He didn't choose the perfect, but rather made them perfect in Him. He will do the same for you!

As our journeys continue, the Lord will guide and direct our lives, taking our imperfections and shaping them to take root. Then, we will see how those beautiful flaws can actually help us find our radiance. Shine bright, Sisters!

Roots

Was there something in your past or present that God used to help you realize your need for Him? Share.

_____

_____

_____

_____

Blooms

From your past, what has God most used to help you relate, empathize, and minister to others?

_____

_____

_____

_____

Prayer

"Lord Jesus, thank You that You take all of me, every flaw. Thank You that You use it all for Your glory. Help me to accept that I can shine because You have chosen to place Your light in my life—for Your glory and ministry to others. In Jesus' name, amen."

Life's journey is
beautifully flawed.

Day 37

PREPARING THE SOIL

The time we spend in preparation is one of the most important and potentially fertile seasons for us as we walk through life in accordance with God's plan. But so often the soil we find ourselves planted in can be dry, lacking the nutrients needed to grow and mature. Yet wherever we may be planted, we can begin to prepare for new roots to grow. Turn up the dirt and dig into the Word of God so He can pour forth all we need, providing us with the key elements to bring about blooms in His time.

So often during these seasons, life can seem dormant. But we must remember what Paul taught in Hebrews 12: we have to run with perseverance the race marked out for us. This means we must stay in training mode like great athletes in competition or the soldiers who protect our freedoms. We need to go through rigorous training to sustain the pace and keep up to finish the race. But if our plates are too full, we will be unable to sustain, leaving us spinning out of control, rather than gaining strength by growing roots.

Some hindrances that can keep us from the good things God has in store are disorganization, lack of sleep, toxic relationships, hormonal imbalance, the inability to say no, and too much entertainment. We all know our list, don't we? As a wife and mother, I work to balance my career, along with being a daughter, friend, and all the other "hats to wear." I can get so wrapped up in my roles that there isn't margin left for leaning into the Lord to prepare and grow mentally, emotionally, and spiritually. Many times, like you, I am just downright tired! That state is a sure way to get off-track and find myself struggling in dry soil.

Lilies, we must practice self-examination by continually asking the tough questions. Evaluating our too-full days, repenting from sin, and fighting destructive behaviors that only bring us down. The truth is that the Lord has planted each of us in His good soil. But like the flowers of the field, we must contribute to improve that soil by submitting to Him in the changes we go through daily.

Sisters, to grow where we have been planted, we must respect our preparation time. We already have the ability. So, as the world-changers that we are, we need to be prepared to take on what the Lord has called us to do. We must be ready to absorb His rich ingredients to bloom where and when we are called in the seasons we enter. Preparation is the training process we undergo to take on whatever lies ahead, readying us for our unique calling, for such a time as this.

Exercise daily in God—no spiritual flabbiness, please! Workouts in the gymnasium are useful, but a disciplined life in God is far more so, making you fit both today and forever. You can count on this. Take it to heart.

1 Timothy 4:8 MSG

Roots

When was a time you knew God had placed you in a season of preparation?

_____

_____

_____

_____

_____

Blooms

What did God do to release you from the preparation? What happened as a result of that time?

_____

_____

_____

_____

_____

Prayer

"Lord Jesus, keep me from distractions. Help me to see all my life and every role I have through the eyes of being Your daughter. Whether preparation, planting, or blooming, I want to stay close to You and take Your truth to heart. In Jesus' name, amen."

Remind yourself every day
that this life is merely
preparation for eternity.

PRECIOUS GEMS

I love precious gems! Whether I'm singing along to the classic Beatles' song, "Lucy in the Sky with Diamonds" or reading stories about princesses adorned with jewels by handsome princes, I imagine the great grandeur of treasures that elevated one's beauty in history; women spoken about in metaphor as rare and exquisite gems, visually stunning to the beholder.

When I was in India, I saw, firsthand, women wearing gemstones laid in gold from the top of their head to their toes. Of course, they love wearing jewelry, but the stones themselves have significant social meaning in their culture. The tradition in the Hindu culture is to enhance one's beauty, while also symbolizing wealth, power, and status. Jewelry is purposefully worn in quality and quantity to draw attention to one's self.

Throughout Scripture, we find mention of brilliant gemstones created by God, representing the twelve tribes of Israel all the way to describing the finishing touches in Heaven. Breathtaking! The Lord knows how to create beautiful things and use them to represent Him and His home.

In Exodus 28, I was taken with the idea that the Lord specifically named the precious stones and gave one to each tribe with precise instructions to those He filled with His spirit and skill to make Aaron's garments to wear for priesthood in "glory and beauty." Called the "Breastplate of Judgment," each stone was given, inscribed, and placed by God. The glorious garment was worn when going before the Lord and praying on behalf of the twelve tribes of Israel. I am captivated by these rich, gleaming gems that were purposed by God.

Of course, God masterfully creates all the stones and gems that we are able to extract from the earth. They go through a process of pressure, bringing the raw and uncut beauties up from the dirt to be used, just like us as His daughters, rough with flaws. These imperfections are labeled by gemologists as "birthmarks" because they are inflicted with major blemishes. Yet God created them, knowing they would go through a process of refinement, not to be perfected, but to be polished to be used for His glory and beauty.

Robert Ludlum, author of the Bourne Trilogy, said, "The most precious jewels are not made of stone, but of flesh." What an incredible visual for us as God's women. A powerful reminder that He created each one of us, and we are more valuable to Him than any precious stone. Our worth, power, and status is not defined by how much we try to enhance and adorn ourselves. Our uncut and raw beauty is defined, shaped, and purposed by God to glorify Him. How much greater are we able to shine from the inside out, holding onto the powerful fact that our flaws tell a story that we can speak to and about, sharing with all those we meet the reason for our sparkle and luster, like precious gems.

And put your gold in the dust,
And the gold of Ophir among the stones of the brooks,
Then the Almighty will be your gold
And abundant silver to you.
For then you will take pleasure in the Almighty
And lift up your face to God.

Job 22:24-26

Roots

What quality or characteristic do you feel God created in you by the "process of pressure" or through a "birthmark" you view as a blemish?

_____

_____

_____

Blooms

How has God used the quality or characteristic you named to minister to others?

_____

_____

_____

Prayer

"Lord Jesus, remind me when I feel like I can't take the pressures of life that You are using them to create something beautiful in me, and for others to see, that reflects You. Remind me to lift my face to You and keep my eyes off the gold and silver of this world. In Your name, amen."

The greater the pressure,
The higher the heat,
The longer in the dark,
The more beautiful the diamond!

Day 39

PROVISION OF ALL GOOD THINGS

"For the Lord God is a sun and shield;
The Lord gives grace and glory;
He withholds no good thing
from those who walk with integrity."

Psalm 84:11

Over the years, I have found that the Lord gives me a word (or words) when He's about to bring a new season into my life. He begins to prepare me for what's to come, whether life pours rain or bright sunshine. He then gently reminds me of that word, inviting me to hang onto Him. Truly, every time a word has come, it has gone hand-in-hand with a new place I enter. For the current year, my word is "provision." Already, the Lord has shown Himself to be faithful. I came into it raising my hands up towards the Great Provider, crying out for rest and peace with a broken spirit in desperate need. He answered and spoke these words to me, "I will provide."

I began to think about all the prayers I had lifted up to Him and, for some reason, all I could see was financial provision. But as I stepped into a new season of life, He started showing up in special ways to fill my longing heart with priceless things money cannot buy. The Lord began to fill me from the inside out, starting with my need for renewed physical, emotional, and spiritual energy that I haven't had for a long time. The Holy Spirit's power began to permeate me to provide a new lease on life throughout my days, bringing me to experience sweet rest at night.

The Lord was feeding me and giving me cool drinks of water, refreshing my soul, showing up everywhere in my life. Like the bridegroom for his bride, His passionate pursuit of me once again rang true to my heart. He was bringing me to a new place, empowering the call on my life through my ministry—The Women in my World—connecting me with old friends, while establishing new ones. Next, He led me to a new church home, His provision pouring forth like new wine.

I once again longed to be the woman God created me to be. In a spirit of transparency, my husband and I have encountered a great deal of external turmoil the past several years, and I was slowly beginning to lose myself. Many times, I was drowning, fighting to keep my head above water. But the trials of this world either make you or break you, and I stay determined to be a fighter through my faith in my heavenly Father, believing His words, "I will provide."

The spirit the Lord has given me is that of a warrior, and I believe the same about you, Sisters. We cannot let the darkness of this world cover up and destroy the light the Lord has placed within us. When we struggle and long to be replenished, we must ask Him to shine bright and move us to experience His provision. Whatever season you may be walking through in your life today, or whatever word the Lord continues to speak to your heart, just lean in, Sisters, and seek the Great Provider. Get ready to watch what He will do to lead you to, as today's passage states, His "grace and glory" because He "withholds no good thing from those who walk with integrity."

Roots

Has there been a difficult season in your life where you desperately prayed for God to give you a word to hang on to? Share.

_____

_____

_____

_____

Blooms

How did God work to bring you out of that season, and how has that made you stronger today?

_____

_____

_____

_____

Prayer

"Lord Jesus, You are my sun and shield. You are my grace and glory. Through my seasons of sadness and celebration, help me to keep my eyes on You to walk in integrity, believing You will withhold no good thing from me. In Jesus' name, amen."

God greets you
with His glory,
grants you His grace,
and gifts you
with the good in this life.

Day 40

THE HARVEST

Toward the end of 2020, we made the decision to leave our home, church, and friends after years in California and move to Georgia. And yes, the departure also meant leaving so many of the women that have been part of my world and who have added such joy to my life, growing me in my walk with Christ, and empowering me to reach for my dreams. Each one a lily that will forever be a part of my colony. The moment we pulled out of our driveway for the last time, the Lord once again reminded me of my calling, not just in California or Georgia, but to *all* women, everywhere.

As I began the process of settling into my new home, I got up early each morning to dig into my devotional time with the Lord, thinking about this next season. One morning, as I sat quietly in front of my fireplace, the Lord led me to the story of Ruth. That book of the Bible has spoken to me many times over the years, a different experience each time, highlighting nuggets of gold for growth in my marriage and, like Ruth with Naomi, in my relationship with my own mother-in-law. So once again, I dug into the powerful story.

As I read, the word "gleaning" kept rising up from the text and speaking directly to my spirit. Boaz allowed Ruth to go in after the reapers to

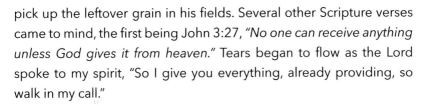

pick up the leftover grain in his fields. Several other Scripture verses came to mind, the first being John 3:27, *"No one can receive anything unless God gives it from heaven."* Tears began to flow as the Lord spoke to my spirit, "So I give you everything, already providing, so walk in my call."

Quickly, I flipped to another verse that came to mind, Galatians 6:10, *"So then, [a]while we have opportunity, let's do good to all people, and especially to those who are of the household of the faith."* I knew right away that the Lord was speaking about my ministry—The Women in my World. Those who love Him! As the excitement grew, I turned to Matthew 9:37, *"The harvest is great but the workers are few"* (NLT).

As I went back to the word "gleaning," I realized that I too was to glean in the spiritual sense, to gather together those who have been left behind. Women who might not have the most followers on social media, or the longest resume, or be seen by the world as "A-list" talent, but women of God, daughters of The Most High who are ready for opportunity.

Ruth knew the value of what the reapers missed, the leftovers in the field. And she was ready to work. She had her eyes on the prize, hoping to find favor with Boaz, the "kinsman" who would redeem her, just like Christ later redeemed His bride. The Lord is so good to give us such powerful stories of His love for us, not wanting us to be left behind, or feel unwanted because of our pasts and flaws, all that is left in our lives to be used by Him, for Him.

Sisters, we are all called into ministry, but so often we have our eyes on bringing the masses to know Jesus, standing in front of the bright lights and stadiums full of people. But just like after the reapers have worked their way through the field, let's not forget all those who remain, those left behind, needing and wanting to be gleaned. So many times, I have felt as though I have been left out in the field, passed over. But our Creator wants to use us to glorify His kingdom. He will not leave His bride behind. He will not leave me. He will not leave you.

As I close this devotional, working in my own new field in this new season, I look forward to gleaning, to encountering more women of God, encouraging and reminding them to keep their eyes on the prize—Jesus, our kinsman redeemer. No matter where we are or where He takes us, God in His grace and sovereignty has placed us there, all for His purposes.

For they are transplanted to the Lord's own house.
They flourish in the courts of our God.

Psalm 92:13 NLT

As we have gone through this devotional together, digging deeper roots, growing and blooming, becoming the women God created us to be, let's now go out into the fields, our communities, work places, schools, wherever He sends us. The harvest is rich and ready to reap. Together, lilies, let's work for the Lord!

Roots

What is one primary truth, principle, or word that God spoke to you in these forty days that you know you need to obey and work into your life?

_____

_____

_____

_____

_____

_____

_____

_____

Blooms

What is one primary truth, principle, or word that God spoke to you that you know He intends you to use to minister to others in His name?

_____

_____

_____

_____

_____

_____

_____

_____

I want to close this final day by praying the words of the apostle Paul over your life and your calling in Christ:

I pray that from his glorious, unlimited resources he will empower you with inner strength through his Spirit. Then Christ will make his home in your hearts as you trust in him. Your roots will grow down into God's love and keep you strong. And may you have the power to understand, as all God's people should, how wide, how long, how high, and how deep his love is. May you experience the love of Christ, though it is too great to understand fully. Then you will be made complete with all the fullness of life and power that comes from God. Now all glory to God, who is able, through his mighty power at work within us, to accomplish infinitely more than we might ask or think. Glory to him in the church and in Christ Jesus through all generations forever and ever! Amen.

Ephesians 3:16-21 NLT

Grow deep,
Reach up,
Reach out,
Live full,
Love strong,
Bloom in beauty.

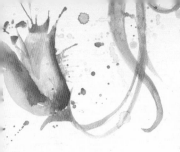

TO THE LILIES

Wow! What a beautiful journey we have taken together. Thank you for joining me for forty days of digging deeper with the Lord and growing roots that will bloom for His glory. I pray that you have encountered the Father on an entirely new level, acquainting yourself with the audacious love He has for you. No wonder the Master Planner created you and me for such a time as this.

I hope as you consumed each day you have been reminded of your identity in Christ—cultivating new ideas and unearthing the woman that the Lord designed you to be—ultimately, getting to know the Savior of the world in a personal relationship that is authentic, transparent, and immeasurable, seeing Him in everything. Whether in a dormant season or in bloom, I pray you have found peace right where He has planted you.

During these forty days of devotion, I pray you have found your colony of women and are working through the checklist of fruit in your life as you have encountered God's creation. On your journey, I believe you will begin to see your life full of joy and abundant fruit.

I would like to close our time together with two personal challenges for you:

First, I want to encourage you to keep going in this daily time of getting to know the Lord, feeling His power as you dive into His Word every day, first thing in the morning, setting your eyes on Him, seeking His will for your life!

Second, to put everything we have discussed into practice, pray about and consider inviting one or two other women in your world to go through these forty days with you. Because you have already walked through the content, you will be able to facilitate the gathering in discussing the application questions, sharing your hearts, and praying for one another. This opportunity will create a beautiful colony as you bloom together.

Thank you, Sisters, for being the amazing Women in my World. Shine bright!

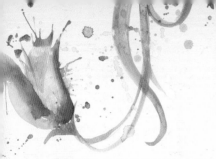

NOTES

NOTES